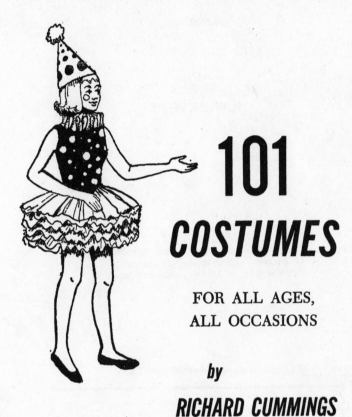

101

COSTUMES

FOR ALL AGES,
ALL OCCASIONS

by

RICHARD CUMMINGS

illustrated by Opal Jackson

Publishers   PLAYS, INC.   *Boston*

First Paperback Edition 1987

Library of Congress Cataloging-in-Publication Data

Cummings, Richard, 1931-
    101 costumes for all ages, all occasions / by Richard
Cummings; illustrated by Opal Jackson. — New ed.
        p.   cm.
    Includes index.
    Summary: A guide to making costumes representative of all
ages or eras and for all occasions.
    ISBN 0-8238-0286-8 (pbk.): $10.00
    1. Costume—Juvenile literature. [1. Costume.] I. Jackson,
Opal, ill. II. Title. III. Title: One hundred one costumes for
all ages, all occasions. IV. Title: One hundred and one costumes
for all ages, all occasions.
PN2067.C85 1987   792'.026—dc19   87-20298 CIP

MANUFACTURED IN THE UNITED STATES OF AMERICA

Contents

Introduction

CLOTHING was undoubtedly first worn for protection from the weather, thorn bushes, and other people, but clothes became costumes the moment a bit of feather, fringe, or fur was added to attract attention — on or off stage. From that use, it was only a short step to the use of costume in masquerades or theatrical productions. The earliest dramatic performances were religious — shamans and witch doctors making magic — but there must also have been costumes simply for entertainments and tomfoolery, as well as for pomp and ceremonials. Since woman first twined a flower in her hair and man first decorated his shield (and his body) with painted signs of his bravery and exploits, costume has been an essential feature in courtship.

Though the materials and styles in costume have varied over the centuries, reflecting local mores, customs, and tastes, "dressing up" has always had a common purpose and motivation: to impress, persuade; to attract attention and to highlight individual characteristics; to set a person apart from others by use of different dress and modes of apparel.

Today there is a wide range of inexpensive, often readily available costume materials. Artificial fibers of every design and color, imitations of expensive silks and velvets, as well as of various furs, can be found in fabric stores. Feathers, betel nut necklaces from Borneo, batik sarongs, imitation leathers, styrofoam for carving masks, sheet foil for armor—all of these can be readily acquired for play productions in school classrooms or assemblies, or for public performances. With a little imagination, almost any desired effect can be achieved.

The foam packing used in the shipping of equipment can be converted into helmets for science fiction characters and monsters; mop handles into spears; dried flowers into decorations for hats and bonnets for period productions; cardboard tubes into telescopes; other materials for many, many more bizarre outfits.

Making costumes from household items is part of the fun of putting on a play, a challenge to ingenuity: burlap, aluminum foil, bottle caps (to make armor and mail when stapled to cloth), cereal boxes — there is really no limit to creating costumes for effective and inexpensive presentation of plays from all countries and all periods of history, and drawing on the artistic as well as the dramatic abilities of young people and amateur actors of all ages. It is for this purpose that this book is presented.

The Costumes

NOVELTY COSTUMES

HISTORICAL GUIDE

(Costumes listed by Number)

NATIONAL FOLK GUIDE

(Costumes listed by Number)

101
COSTUMES

Instant
Costumes

THESE COSTUMES can be put together—well nearly—in an instant. No cutting or sewing required. All you need are a few things found around the house, such as safety pins, string, sewing scraps, towels, sheets and old clothes. Have a minute? Try this:

1. INSTANT FRANKENSTEIN

Wet your hair against your forehead so that it forms the famous Frankenstein fringe. (For more complete make-up on this and other occasions, see the author's *101 Masks*). For the costume, find an old suit coat, preferably a bit large for you, and dull colored. Put it on backwards, have somebody button you up behind, thrust out your arms, scowl ferociously, and move toward your victim with stiff-legged, menacing walk. Flee for your lives—the Monster!

2. INSTANT NAPOLEON

Find an old fedora or man's felt hat and pin the brim up, front and back, then attach a paper or whisk broom cockade in front. Turn the lapels of an old coat upward and across, then pin the bottom front corners back. Add a sash

of wide ribbon or crepe paper and a few tin-foil medals. Now thrust your left hand inside the coat and strike an imperial pose. Who's daffy?

3. INSTANT GHOST

You make a ghost from a bed sheet, anyone knows that. Secure the outside edges around your wrists with rubber bands, as shown on Pg. 3. Cut eye holes at least an inch and a half wide for maximum visibility. To scare the wits out of old Scrooge in Dickens' *A Christmas Carol*, drape Marley's ghost in chains and locks and paint old cigar boxes to look like cash boxes. If that doesn't straighten the old miser out, show him the Ghost of Christmas Future, staring out of a shadowed hood, folded from a sheet.

4. INSTANT MAN-AT-ARMS

To become a common spear-holder for a period play or historical pageant, you need coat, hat and sheet. Roll your trousers above the knee and drape the coat in front as an apron-tunic, tying the sleeves around behind. Tie the sheet on as a cape, knotting it loosely around your neck. For a spear, attach a cardboard or papier-mâché point to a broomstick. (See *Making Weapons*, Pg. 62.) You can wear an old pair of boots, or elaborate a pair of sandals with leggings of criss-crossed clothesline rope, dressmaker's tape or leather bootlaces. (See *Converting Footgear*, Pg. 98.) Or you can stand guard barefoot. For headgear, convert an old hat into a fifteenth century sallet helmet by tucking the front half of the brim up inside and leaving the other half out at the back.

Hat Folding

This is a traditional "quick turn" of vaudeville. Use a man's fedora or a woman's broad-brimmed hat of good quality felt,

A   B   C

D   E   F

flexible but firm-bodied, with a brim at least 2½ inches wide. It can be folded into a variety of shapes, such as A, Comedian; B, Robin Hood; and C, Jester. Of, if you have the time and money, you can make the French folding hat, called *Le Chapeau Magique*. Cut out a large circular brim of quality felt, in the dimensions shown. With practice, it can be manipulated into dozens of shapes, including those shown: D, Dutch Maiden; E, Lord Nelson; and F, The Flying Nun.

5. INSTANT ORIENTAL

If your pajamas aren't oriental enough, add a mandarin collar of black paper and button loops or frogs, as shown. The pigtail is made from an old nylon stocking, cut lengthwise from the foot in three strips and braided. Make a skullcap out of a tube of black crepe paper gathered with rubber bands or string, then trimmed with scissors, as shown. For footwear, ballet or bedroom slippers will do. (For more authentic Chinese and Japanese dress, see Costumes No. 79 and No. 82.)

6. EGYPTIAN SLAVE

The Egyptians wove linen and probably made some of the earliest cloth clothing, replacing the animal skins worn before. The lowliest men among them wore the simplest garment, the loincloth. Fold a single bedsheet four times lengthwise, or cut a narrow rectangle 2½ by about 6½ feet. (Or two large towels can be pinned or sewed together, end to end.) Begin by wrapping the cloth around the hips or loins, crossing the two ends in front. One end is brought up behind the other, then over to form the draped panel in front. The other end is taken down through the legs, up behind the hips, and tucked into the waist at the back. A later modification of this basic garment was the draped and pleated skirt, made from a large rectangle of sheeting, wrapped around the hips, gathered up in front and looped

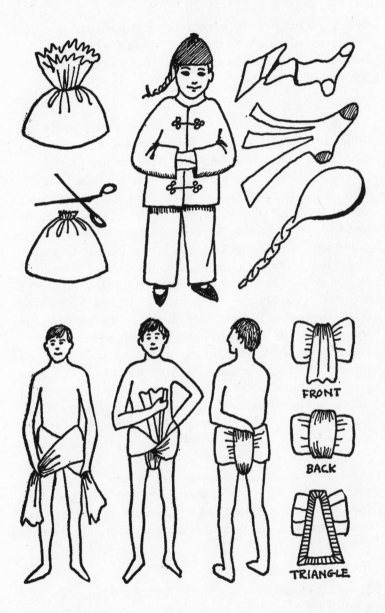

FRONT

BACK

TRIANGLE

over a belt or girdle to drape in front. A decorated triangular tab was often attached to hang in front, as shown in the bottom right-hand corner of the illustration. Egyptian slaves usually went barefoot.

7. GREEK LADY

The garments of Greece's Golden Age were essentially the same for men and women. They were often fastened with pins rather than sewed, and they were neither shaped nor fitted, but were draped to fall in dead folds upon the body. This early Doric *chiton*, also called *peplos*, is made from a simple rectangle of wool, linen or silk. Its classical measurements were: double the distance from elbow to elbow (measured with the arms spread), or a few inches wider; by from one foot to eighteen inches more than the wearer's height. A large bed sheet is about the right size and can be adjusted by holding it against the body and folding the extra length over in front until the sheet reaches from the shoulders to the floor, as shown. Next, the garment is put around the body, with the open side on the right, and pinned over each shoulder, back over front. A well-worn sheet will drape better than a new one. A belt or girdle of ribbon can be added to lift the bodice up and give a blousing effect in front. The men often wore their chitons shorter, leaving the legs exposed. Greeks often went barefoot, but also wore sandals. (See *Making Footgear*, Pg. 102.) The ancient Greeks were not so fond of white and pastel-colored fabrics as is commonly assumed. The sheet used to make the chiton can be dyed one of their favorite colors: indigo, yellow, violet, dark red, or dark purple. (See *Dyeing Fabrics*, Pg. 70.)

8. INSTANT CAVE MAN

Here is the easiest costume of all, if you happen to have a bit of fur around the house. If not, what about a swatch

of brown, gray, black or white flannelette or fuzzy-napped cloth? Flannelette can be dyed and brushed up into a furry nap while wet. (See *Dyeing Fabrics*, Pg. 70.) The cave man's club can be any old tree branch; or a comically bulbous club can be made from papier-mâché. (See *Papier-mâché*, Pg. 42.)

9. INSTANT OATMEAL

For this quick novelty costume, cut head and arm holes in a pasteboard box, preferably one that has contained boxes of oatmeal and is already decorated. Or the box can be painted, as shown. Construct a tubular container and paint a smiling Quaker on it, and you are dressed as yet another brand. Use a garden spade for a giant spoon, or make one by attaching an oval of cardboard to a length of broomstick.

10. INSTANT SIAMESE TWINS

One outsized dress with two girls inside it and a sheet rolled and wrapped around them as padding makes a pretty funny side show monstrosity for a comic pageant or backyard circus. Two boys in a giant pair of pants give a similar effect. (See Novelty Costumes and Index for other circus get-ups.)

The Riddling Twins

For your first costume "show," have the twins do a comic routine, asking one another riddles or indulging in other vaudeville nonsense, such as:

Twin: How do you drive a baby buggy?
Twin: Tickle his feet.

11. INSTANT OLIVER TWIST

Here is Dickens' tattered ragamuffin, costumed in a jiffy

with scraps and castoffs from the household rummage bag. To make rents or tears in material, start with a scissors cut, tear the rest of the way by hand, and, if you wish, scorch the frayed edges with a hot iron. Patches can be made in a hurry from iron-on fabric. From the same ragbag you can costume a hobo, a gypsy, a tramp clown. Trousers can be so large they threaten to fall, gloves so small the fingers thrust free. The more extreme the misfit, the more comic the effect. (See No. 52 for costuming the Tramp Clown.)

Rummage Bag Costumes

A great variety of quick costumes can be put together from fabric remnants, cast-off clothing and odd accessories. Check the basement, attic and garage for possibilities, including shoes, hats, jewelry, canes and weapons. Try the neighbors, second-hand stores and the thrift shops run by the Salvation Army, Goodwill Industries and St. Vincent de Paul. Women's hats come in every shape and color, ready to be converted to countless uses. Watch for old furs, bags, belts, and used military equipment. Most of the items worn by the Flapper in the illustration can be found in a modern wardrobe, and can be given the Roaring Twenties finish with the addition of fringe, beads, and ostrich feathers. The cloche can be made from the crown of an old fedora, with the band removed and the front edge turned up. Her brash boyfriend, the Masher, wears currently popular bell-bottomed trousers, striped blazer, and wide, wild tie. A plain cane can be painted to look like bamboo, or a comically flexible cane can be made by stringing spools on a strip of inner tubing, drawn tight to hold the spools in line. A passable banjo can be made out of a candy box and scrap wood or a pie tin. (See *Making Musical Instruments*, Pg. 68.) If a straw hat or boater is not available, one can be made from cardboard by the tab and glue method. (See *Making Hats*, Pg. 28.) Flapper and Masher can be a vaudeville song and dance team. With variations, they can

also be a Prohibition couple with the Masher as a well-dressed gangster, and the Flapper as his sultry gun moll.

A few yards of brightly printed fabric wrapped around and tucked in at the top are all the costumes needed for the Samoan Boy and Girl. The flowered leis around their necks can be made from paper flowers or crepe paper. (See No. 19.) They also wear flowers in their hair. The Samoan Boy holds a conch shell, into which he blows to signal other fishermen. Fur-lined winter parkas provide the basic garments for the Eskimo Boy and Girl, with heavy trousers of flannelette or fur added, and shoes called *mukluks* made of dark cloth and tied to the feet and ankles with rope, string, or leather shoestrings. If you are lucky and your rummage bag contains embroidered strips or ribbon, attach them to the parkas as decoration.

Rainy Day Costumes

HERE IS a way to fill a rainy day with fun. Put together some costumes and give a show or produce a pageant at home. Many of these costumes are combinations and conversions of clothes you are likely to have around the house. There will be only a little basic sewing and cutting to do, and no really complicated patterns. As for other materials—scraps of cloth and yarn, cardboard, glue, safety pins, needle and thread—do you have them? Then let's go!

12. SARAH

Sarah wears two basic garments requiring a minimum of sewing. Her outer cloak is the ancient Semitic *aba.* (See No. 13.) Under it, she wears a full-length tunic, modeled after the Greek Ionic chiton. The Ionic chiton does not have the Doric's overfold at the top. It can be made from a simple rectangle, wrapped around the body and sewed at each shoulder, A and B, and down the open side, C. Decorative borders can be tacked on at top and bottom. A belt or girdle and harness can be worn to hold the top in place, as shown, D. Or the tunic can be draped from an old sheet, with a few stitches at one shoulder, E, and a

safety pin holding the other, F. When tying the girdle around the waist, raise both arms overhead, to insure freedom of movement. The garment can fall all the way to the floor, but if it is to be worn on the stage, it is best to cut it short of the tops of the feet, to prevent tripping over the hem. Sarah's headdress can be a simple shawl or large kerchief, but Hebrew women also wore elaborate arrangements of braids and gold coin jewelry. (See *Making Jewelry*, Pg. 53.)

13. ABRAHAM

While wandering in the wilderness, the Hebrew elder wore a simple tunic much like his wife's, and a heavy aba or outer cloak. The aba was sometimes as much as nine feet wide, but you can make a less voluminous basic cloak from a sheet or blanket, folded in from either side, as shown, B, and sewed over the shoulders. The aba was most often made of a heavy material, usually wool. Burlap sacking or monk's cloth can be used. (See *Inexpensive Fabrics*, Pg. 20). Woven goat or camel's hair fabric can be simulated with dyed and brushed flannelette. (See *Dyeing Fabrics*, Pg. 70.) The Hebrew version of the aba often had wide stripes of alternating colors. Flannel sheeting comes in stripes, as do awning material and mattress ticking; or you can loosely sew or baste strips of colored material to a blanket or sheet. Abraham's beard can be made from a clean yarn mop, or it can be more elaborate. (See *Making Beards and Wigs*, Pg. 50.) He wears the traditional head cloth of the wandering Arab tribes, still worn by the modern Bedouin. It is usually made from a large square of white wool, but can be made from a pillow case, dish towel or bath towel, and is held in place, as shown, A, by a round

A

B

"tire" of decorative cord or cloth strips, twisted or braided.
His staff can be a broomstick or trimmed tree branch.

14. PETER PAN

The boy who can't grow up wears green tights and a long-
tailed shirt of harmonizing color, belted at the waist like
a tunic. The collar can be cut off or folded inside and the
opening laced across with string or thongs. The hat is made
from the crown of an old fedora, turned up and trimmed
with a feather, real or cut from cardboard. Wear bedroom
slippers, or, to make cuffed and pointed shoes, see *Converting Footgear*, Pg. 98.

15. TINKER BELL

Although she is often presented as only a tiny light, Tinker
can also be dressed as a visible fairy, as shown here. Her
dress can be a pretty party gown or can be made from a
curtain of fine nylon net or double-ply cheesecloth, cut like
a Mexican serape, dropped over the head and gathered at
the waist with a tie of pastel-colored ribbon. The simplest
wings are made of wire and covered with fine net or
cheesecloth, glued or sewed in place.

Inexpensive Fabrics

When choosing a cheap material to imitate a more expensive
fabric, consider the weight, quality of sheen and draping
characteristics. Among the materials which drape well are
cheesecloth (made up double), Japanese cotton crepe, cotton
voile (for veils and scarves), Canton flannel or flannelette,
sateen and satinette, and pongee. Heavy flannelette, burlap,
corduroy and terry cloth also drape fairly well, and have body
and weight. Gingham, dimity and percale are stiff and lightweight. For stiffness with body and weight, use unbleached
muslin or cheap canvas. For the high sheen of silks and satins,

use glazed cambric, silkoline, nylon or rayon. Deep-colored Canton flannel makes a good substitute for velvet, as do flannelette and terry cloth, when properly dyed. (See *Dyeing Fabric,* Pg. 70.) Woolen garments can be reproduced with woolen batiste, flannelette, muslin or even burlap, monk's cloth or tobacco cloth. Crepe paper can be used for costumes to be worn only sparingly. Sew or paste it with the grain going in the direction in which you want it to hang. (For further suggestions, see *Esoteric Costume Materials,* Pg. 182, and *Special Fabrics,* Pg. 92.)

16. CAPTAIN HOOK

This prancing pirate wears an old suit coat with claw-hammer tails sewed on at the back. At his throat are crepe paper ruffles stapled or sewed to a child's bib or right onto the shirt. His breeches are only trousers tucked up and held in place below the knee by long black stockings and rubber bands or sewed elastic. His hat is an old fedora with a feather, real or paper, added. Cardboard buckles are painted white or silver and tied over the laces of a pair of black oxfords. The mustache can be cut out of cardboard and attached to a false nose, or can be more elaborate. (See *Making Beards and Wigs,* Pg. 50.) The hook at the end of his right arm is made from cardboard or a bent wire coat hanger, fixed to a bell-shaped guard of masking tape or cardboard and gripped from inside by the hidden right hand. The rest of the pirate crew wears a variety of gear, with trousers shredded at the bottom, eye patches of black cloth or paper, earrings, sashes, head scarves, and wooden cutlasses. (See *Making Battle Weapons,* Pg. 62.) Captain and crew are shown performing in a living room production of *Peter Pan.*

Putting On a Show at Home

A living room entrance arch makes a good proscenium for a home stage; or you can use the back end of a garage or a corner of the basement. Rig curtains or use folding screens. Floor lamps can be used as spotlights for dramatic lighting effects. Music can be live or by phonograph. Weapons should be blunted whenever possible, and the use of real firearms should be avoided. (See *Making Firearms*, Pg. 126.) If you plan to make a pageant of the Peter Pan story, remember that pageants are best staged out of doors, in the yard or on a large porch. (See *Presenting a Pageant*, Pg. 37.)

17. RUSSIAN MAN

Here is your first national or "folk" costume, actually the dress of a nineteenth century Georgian peasant. The white smock can be made from an outsized man's shirt or a full-sleeved woman's blouse, trimmed with brightly colored borders, as shown. Any billed hat of a darker color can be used, or one can be made. (See *Making Hats*, Pg. 28.) Full trousers of a dark color are tucked into the tops of boots, or into leggings made of black plastic sheeting or oilcloth matched to a pair of dark shoes. (See *Converting Footgear*, Pg. 98.) The leggings can be sewed on or secured at the back with elastic.

18. BALKAN WOMAN

She is wearing the native dress of the Ukraine and could be the wife of the Russian man. The key garments of the costume can often be found as part of the modern wardrobe: the full-sleeved "peasant blouse," the full skirts and petticoats, and the kerchief headdress. Either slippers or boots can be worn. The same basic costume, with variations in detail, serves as the female folk dress of Roumania,

Yugoslavia, Austria and Italy. Skirts can be filled out with petticoats made of crepe paper. Winged and shaped head-dresses can be made from stiff cambric or buckram. (See No. 78.) Costume decorations include braided belts, embroidered aprons, embroidered borders and flowers, and variously colored flowered or striped print fabrics sewed in strips or panels.

19. WAHINI LOA

Few islanders ever wore the grass skirt as everyday dress, but it is a part of the popular picture of Pacific Islands costume. The top can be made from a halter or swimming suit top. The skirt can be made of raffia or narrow crepe paper strips attached to a waistband or belt. The waistband can be decorated with buttons in imitation of cowrie shells. Cellophane strips swing more sinuously from a dancer's hips than do raffia or crepe paper. The flower leis can be made from strung crepe paper rosettes. Or you can cut a strip of crepe paper about 1½ inches wide and several yards long. Gather it lengthwise through the middle with needle and thread, A, then twist it on the thread until it kinks up into a series of rosettes, B, which can be cut to length and tied into a necklace. Or you can string paper or plastic flowers. Hula dancers most often dance barefooted.

20. AFRICAN WITCH DOCTOR

This costume is similar to that worn by witch doctors in Central Africa, but a great number of variations exist. Skin decorations are made with non-toxic body paint. (See *Body Paint*, Pg. 178.) A mantle of bunched straw or raffia is tied and hung from the shoulders like a cape. A head-dress is made out of feathers or dry grass or raffia, sewed or stapled to a decorated headband. A rattle can be made

A

B

from a dried gourd or a baking powder or other can, containing dried beans, and fixed to a wooden handle. Dime store sleigh bells can be attached to a belt or to raffia leg decorations, to jingle while the doctor dances. Also shown is a body mask worn by African dancers, made from a large cone of cardboard. For the standard masquerade party "cannibal," you can dye a pair of long johns or tights and a T-shirt and darken face, hands and feet with burnt cork. The bone in the nose is carved out of some light wood such as pine or balsa and attached to a length of wire bent so as to pinch the septum of the nose and hold the bone in place. African dance masks can be made from papier-mâché or Claycrete. (See *Papier-mâché*, Pg. 42. For African dance mask designs and instructions, consult the author's *101 Masks*.)

21. WICKED WITCH

This old hag can appear in the tale of Snow White, in a play about Sleeping Beauty, or she can be one of the unpleasant sisters in Cinderella. (For a more fanciful woman of menace, see the Design chapter, ahead.) She wears a circular cloak or cape, cut after the basic pattern shown. For a broom, wire a bundle of twigs to a trimmed branch. Her high conical hat has a wide brim and can be made from black construction paper or cardboard covered with cloth.

Making Hats

This basic tab-and-glue construction can be used to put together a variety of homemade hats. In each case, the brim or the visor should be made of heavyweight construction board to prevent warping. The body of the hat is best made from good quality Bristol board, lighter and more flexible, so that the tabs can be bent and glued without breaking. Tabs can also be cut into the bottom edge of the hat body, also bent and also glued, for double strength. If possible, make each hat from construction materials of the desired color, gluing with white glue, which dries clear and will not seriously mar the color. If the hat is to be painted, it is best to paint the parts before gluing, pressing them flat during the drying process, to avoid warping. Cloth covering is best added after the hat has been constructed. Texture, such as the roughness on a straw boater, can be added with papier-mâché or Claycrete, brushed on in a thin layer, combed and allowed to dry, then painted. The rounded crown of the derby can be finished off smoothly with papier-mâché or Claycrete. Before deciding to make your own hat, be sure to check your local thrift shop to see if there is not a cast-off woman's hat which can be converted to your purpose by judicious trimming or removal of excess decoration. To convert a fedora to a top hat, see No. 59.

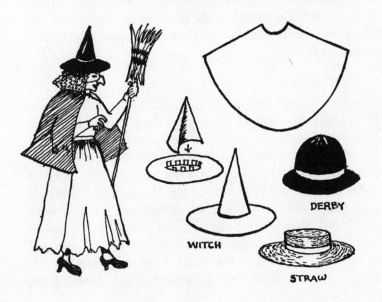

WITCH

DERBY

STRAW

22. PRISCILLA MORGAN

The costume of the Puritans was essentially the same as that worn by the Roundheads or followers of Oliver Cromwell in seventeenth century England. The colors were warmer than is generally assumed. Priscilla's gown can be black or gray or it can be orange-brown, deep purple or russet. Her doublet can be made from a pajama top, with the side seams loosened, then lapped over the back to tighten the waist. Full petticoats can be made from straight lengths of cambric or muslin stitched together and gathered into waistbands. The full white apron can be made from cotton sheeting or muslin. The collar and cuffs of the tunic should be made of cambric or heavy lawn and cut from the patterns indicated, A. The collar is held together in front by two ribbons or tapes, as shown. The bonnet is made from a dark colored muslin and a turned back section of white cambric basted to the front edge, the bonnet fastened by tapes tied under the chin. Shoes should be heavy, plain and dark.

23. JOHN ALDEN

The doublet and trousers of the Puritan man can be made from a pair of pajamas, dyed gray, deep brown or russet. Collar and cuffs are cut after the patterns, B. Imitation silver or pewter buttons secure the doublet and the outside seams of the trousers legs, with one-inch ribbons or tapes gathering the trousers below the knees. The socks are woolen and usually green. Dark oxfords can be fitted with cardboard tongues. Buckles of wood or cardboard can be painted with radiator paint to simulate silver, or wrapped in foil and attached to the shoes. Similar buckles are attached to belt and hatband. (For the hat, see *Making Hats*,

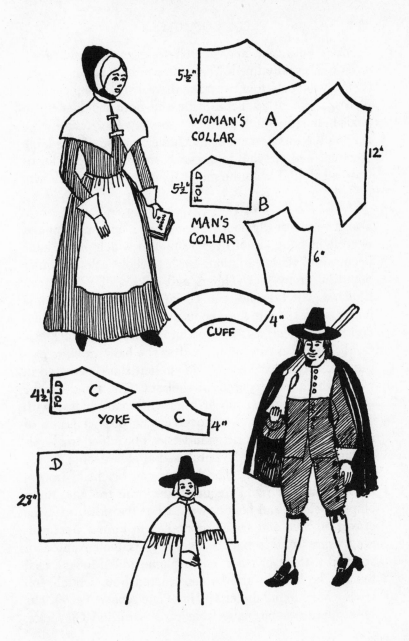

5½"

WOMAN'S
COLLAR   A

12"

5½" FOLD

B

MAN'S
COLLAR

6"

CUFF   4"

4½" FOLD   C

YOKE   C   4"

D

28"

Pg. 28.) Both men and women wear voluminous capes, often red, usually lined. The cape can be made of muslin or heavy flannelette. First make the yoke, C. Then cut four pieces, D, about 28 inches wide and from shoulder tip to ankle in length. Stitch the four pieces together, lengthwise, leaving the fourth seam open. Gather the top of this large rectangle and attach it to the yoke, so that it drapes downward all around, with the single opening in front, as shown.

24. CAPT. JOHN SMITH

The governor of Plymouth Colony was a military man and wore light body armor over a uniform which might have been worn, with variation, by his fellow colonist Miles Standish, or by foot soldiers and officers of Elizabethan England. His breeches can be knickerbockers or pajama bottoms, tucked into knee boots made of oilcloth (see *Converting Footgear*, Pg. 98), or into heavy wool stockings. Or the breeches can be made after the basic trousers pattern illustrated for costume No. 46, cut short, gathered in at the thigh and secured with elastic. The tunic can be made from a pajama top or from a woman's blouse with short puffed sleeves, worn over a long-sleeved jersey of matching color. Cambric gauntlets can be added to gloves, or gauntlet gloves can be purchased at a gardening supply store and dyed black. The helmet can be made from a fedora, with the band removed, the brim trimmed to an ellipsoid shape and bent downward at the sides, with the crown pinched and sewed or stapled to form a crest running from front to back. The whole is then painted or sprayed with silver paint, and a plume added for the final touch. The hat can also be constructed from scratch, following hints found under *Making Plate Armor*, Pg. 40. The breastplate can be made from cardboard and Claycrete,

9"

8" 36"

46"

also following instructions on Page 40. Around his neck, Capt. Smith wears a cambric or lace ruff. (To make, see No. 49.) Miles Standish and other Puritan men-at-arms wear the plain cambric collar and cuffs worn by John Alden, No. 23. Instead of plain breeches, Elizabethan soldiers and officers wore breeches of red slashed with blue or yellow. Somewhat more elaborate but essentially similar uniforms are suitable for the great soldiers, explorers and conquistadores of sixteenth and seventeenth century Spain: Cortez, Pizarro, De Soto. Add a large velveteen beret with a feather, and a straight, sleeveless cloak, and you have the costume of the great Italian navigator, Christopher Columbus.

25. POCAHONTAS

This pretty maiden wears a generalized version of the costume worn by women of a number of North American Indian tribes. The basic garment can be a simple one-piece dress, dyed the brown of deerskin, or can be made of heavy unbleached muslin, cambric (unglazed side outward), or denim, following the basic dress pattern shown. The bottom edge is slashed at half inch intervals to make a fringe 2½ inches long. Sleeves are elbow length, with fringe attached under each arm. Because the natural contour of the skins was preserved, the dress was usually much shorter in the front and back than at the sides. In addition to the fringe, long thongs can be attached to the front of the dress at regular intervals. To simulate the bands of beadwork across the breast, attach strips of cotton decorated with watercolor or felt pen, or use strips of real beadwork. Bead necklaces and a silver belt can be added. Simple leggings of dyed muslin with simulated beadwork can be held in place with elastic. If ready-made moccasins are not available, make a pair, following the pattern given under *Making Footgear*, Pg. 102. Pocahontas wore her hair in braids, but older women preferred to wear their hair loose.

26. CHIEF POWHATAN

Pocahontas' father wears a generalized male Indian costume, not strictly authentic, but similar to the hunting shirt and breeches worn by the braves of many tribes. Pajama top and bottom may be used, or the two garments can be made of muslin or denim, following the patterns, A and B, for a basic shirt and basic breeches. The breeches pattern represents only one leg, folded, with the seam to the rear. Simple leggings can also be made, after the pattern, C, and are suspended by tapes from a belt which also supports a breechcloth, hidden by the tails of the shirt. The shirt should reach halfway to the wearer's knees. The fringed yoke is added separately and decorated with simulated beadwork. The outside edge of each leg can be decorated with fringe or bits of rabbit fur to simulate ermine tails. For the bow and arrow, see *Making Battle Weapons*, Pg. 62. Over his shoulders or attached to his belt, the Chief can wear scalps as trophies, made from bits of fur or tufts of hair, wrapped in beadwork or colored yarn and hung like tassels, or stretched across round twig frames. Strips of bright red and yellow yarn can be braided into the Chief's hair or wig. He is shown here with only a few eagle feathers (turkey or chicken feathers with their ends dipped in brown ink), but on ceremonial occasions, he might wear the full-feathered war bonnet. (See No. 75.) That, however, is no rainy day project and comes under the heading of Advanced Costuming. In the meantime, why not crown your rainy day activities with a Thanksgiving Pageant?

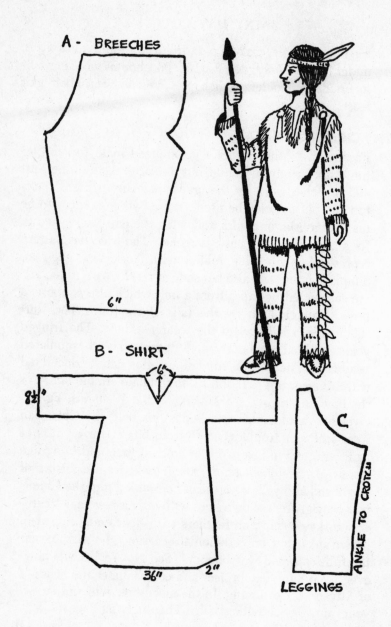

A - BREECHES

6"

B - SHIRT

6"

8½"

36"   2"

C

ANKLE TO CROTCH

LEGGINGS

Presenting a Pageant

The easiest pageants are those which can be presented out of doors, in a ready-made natural setting. If possible, choose an area with a fixed background, such as a wall, fence or screen of trees. Limit your audience to the area immediately opposite the staging area, to prevent them from mingling with the costumed mummers of your pageant. Pageants should be staged in pantomime, with little or no lines spoken by the mummers. Music should be used, live or recorded, to fill in the sound vacuum. Pageants should move, parade-like, across the audience view, hopefully emerging from behind screening "wings" at either side, either artificial, such as garden gates or walls or screens, or natural, such as hedges or clumps of trees. For your Thanksgiving Pageant, you can simply have your costumed Puritans and Indians parade onto the stage and sit down to the first Thanksgiving dinner; or you can elaborate the tale, first by staging John Alden's awkward marriage proposal to Priscilla Morgan on behalf of the shy Miles Standish, followed by the timely intervention of Pocahontas just as Chief Powhatan is about to have Capt. John Smith's head cut off; the whole performance concluding in truce, the parade of Indians bearing turkeys and squash for the table, and the final prayers and solemn celebration of the Thanksgiving feast. History has been scrambled a bit to put together the foregoing version, but history often has to be bent a little to give a pageant the necessary drama. To locate the several other pageant possibilities scattered throughout this book, consult the index under "pageant."

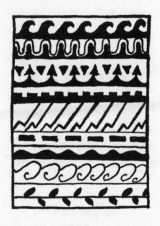

Advanced Costumes

THESE ARE costumes for use in home, school and church entertainments, for community parades and pageants, and for use on the professional stage. The list includes simpler projects and some rather difficult creations. Most are suitable for home or party use, providing the costumer can afford the expense of materials, minimal in some cases, somewhat high in others; and that he has the time needed and the sewing and other skills required. Scattered throughout are rough patterns for basic garments which can be used for other costumes in the book, or for costumes of the reader's own design.

27. ACHILLES

This legendary Greek hero wears strap and plate armor over a short, sewed Doric chiton. (See No. 7 and No. 12.) His helmet can be made from a modified and painted felt fedora, see No. 24, or constructed of cardboard and papier-mâché, see No. 25. For security and convenience, the chiton can be draped in the traditional way, but permanently sewed down the side and at one shoulder. The thong leggings of the sandals can be made from tape or rawhide boot thongs or simulated with black elastic. (See

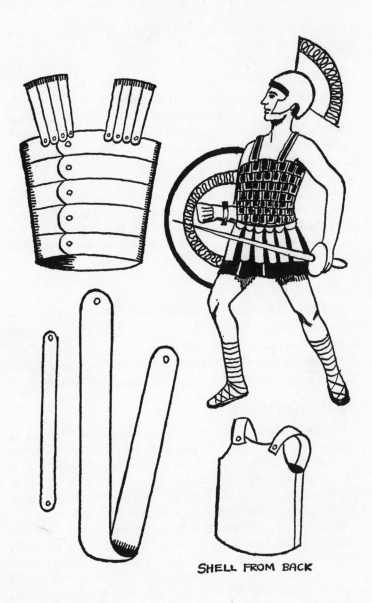

SHELL FROM BACK

Converting Footgear, Pg. 98.) For Achilles' sword, see *Making Battle Weapons,* Pg. 62.

Making Strap Armor

The overlapping straps of Greek and Roman armor were originally made of leather or metal. They may be cut from stiff cambric, Bristol board, leather, leatherette, heavy vinyl, heavy aluminum foil or thin sheet metal. They are then bent to shape and sewed or attached one over the other by rivets or metal eyelets to an undervest of leather or stout canvas, with the skirt plates hanging free from the waist. Or they can be attached to a hard shell patterned after the solid breastplate ahead (No. 28). Or the pattern of the upper plates can be painted directly onto such a hard shell, with only the skirt plates actually cut and riveted in place.

28. HECTOR

According to romantic tradition, this Trojan warrior was killed by Achilles during the siege of Troy. He also wears a short Ionic chiton (see No. 7), but his solid plate armor (breastplate and shin guards) is constructed from Bristol board and papier-mâché, as are his shield and helmet.

Making Plate Armor

Similar methods and materials are employed for making both helmets and solid plate armor. Although chain-mail armor is easier and cheaper to make (see *Making Chain Mail,* Pg. 60), it was not worn by the Greeks or Romans. Plate armor was worn in Greece and Rome and was also common through the Middle Ages and right up to the advent of firearms.

First, the basic foundation of each piece must be cut and formed to the body of the wearer. Buckram can be easily shaped to fit the forearms and shins, A and B, and some pieces can be cut from heavy construction board. For the more difficult chest plate, a cardboard shell must first be made. Cut the form, C, from strong, flexible construction paper or Bristol

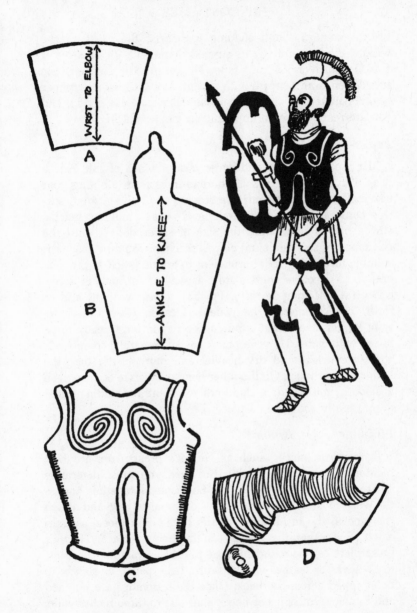

A

WRIST TO ELBOW

B

ANKLE TO KNEE

C

D

board, measuring and shaping it against the chest of the wearer, then reenforcing its cupped shape with glued strips of Bristol board or masking tape, D. Temporarily support the foundation from beneath with a mound of wadded newspaper or other material (plasticine or modeling clay are good), and you are ready to begin applying the papier-mâché.

Papier-mâché

Mix a paste of flour and water. Add a pinch of salt. Add a drop of formaldehyde to discourage mice from nibbling your armor. Cook until the mixture reaches the boiling point, stirring constantly to avoid scorching. To make molding mâché, stir in bits of newspaper the size of silver dollars until the constancy of soft modeling clay is reached. Molding mâché is suitable for adding relief ornament to armor (such as the decoration on Hector's chest plate), as well as for making accessories (see *Making Jewelry*, Pg. 53), tools, weapons and so forth. The commercial equivalent is called Claycrete or Instant Papier-mâché and is purchased dry in bags, ready to be mixed with water. However, most such commercial compounds contain concrete and dry heavier and more brittle than the homemade product. On the other hand, Claycrete can be given a smooth finish and is therefore excellent for adding relief decoration to the finished piece

Finishing Plate Armor

Plate armor pieces, such as Hector's breastplate, are best reenforced with strip mâché. But first, you must determine where and how the pieces will be fastened together and to the wearer's body. Sew small rings of metal to tape and attach the tape to the inside edge of the foundation piece, as indicated, F, so that the pieces can be tied in place. Hector's breastplate can be designed to tie to another plate at the back, to a canvas or leather vest or fabric back panel, or simply to be strapped across the back. Once the fastenings are planned and in place, cut strips of newspaper one to three inches wide,

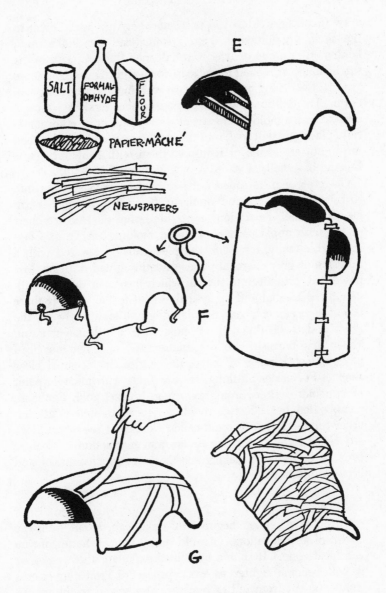

SALT

FORMAL-DPHYDE

FLOUR

PAPIER-MÂCHÉ

NEWSPAPERS

E

F

G

draw them through cooked paste and begin to apply them to the shell, criss-crossing them systematically to build up a laminated skin one quarter to a half inch thick, G. Dry in the sun or in a warm oven for at least forty-eight hours. The more gradual the drying process, the less warping and shrinking will occur. To additionally protect your pieces against warping, dry them on a molded support of wadded paper or other material (plasticine will soak into the mâché or even melt if placed in too hot an oven), or reenforce them with temporary cross bracing of pencils or chopsticks while they dry, E.

Claycrete can be rolled out like bread dough and cut into strips, applied and dried similarly. Once dry, the pieces can be given relief decoration (note the design on Hector's chest plate) with application of sculpted molding mâché or Claycrete, H. Finally, for color, the piece can be covered with a thin skin of gray charcoal paper smoothly glued in place. Mix powdered graphite into shellac which has been thinned with denatured alcohol and apply a thin coat to the shell. If there is raised ornament, rub powdered graphite directly on the relief and touch the highest spots with a little silver paint. When dry, burnish with the smooth part of a hammer-head or any smooth piece of metal, and add a final coat of clear shellac. For easier finishing, merely paint with metallic paint of the color desired: iron-gray, silver, bronze, gold. For more complicated but effective molding processes, investigate another commercial compound called Celastic. (See the author's *101 Hand Puppets* for description and instructions.) Celastic can also be used for making accessories, weapons, masks, and props of all kinds.

Making Helmets

To make a helmet, begin with a skullcap, I, cut from the crown of an old fedora. (An old derby is even better, if you can locate one.) It should be a little large for the wearer, as it will become tighter as work proceeds. Projecting pieces should be cut from felt or buckram and sewed to the cap, J.

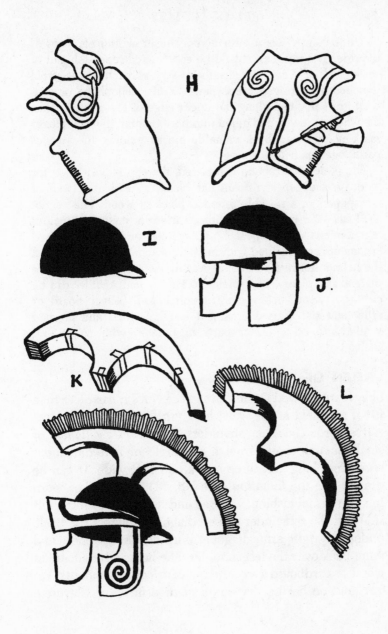

H

I

J.

K

L

Hector's helmet has a visor across the brow and ear flaps at the side. The top crest should be constructed separately out of cardboard or very stiff cambric, K. A roach made from bunched and fringed crepe paper, raffia, cellophane or artificial grass is glued along the upper edge of the crest, L, then the whole is sewed and glued into position atop the cap. Heavy masking tape can be a valuable aid in holding the various parts together before gluing.

The basic construction completed, the cap is positioned for work on a cheap styrofoam hat block, a head-sized wad of newspapers or a suitably rounded block of wood. The helmet shell can then be built up with a variety of materials, including homemade papier-mâché, Claycrete, or Celastic. Raised ornament can be added with molding mâché or Claycrete, and the helmet finished and colored as indicated, above, for other plate armor pieces. The shields of Hector and Achilles can be cut from wood, heavy construction board, beaver board or other material. Raised ornament can be added and finished similarly to other armor parts or painted with colors and shellacked.

29. HELEN OF TROY

She wears a sewed Doric chiton (see No. 7), narrower than usual and held at the waist by a girdle of ribbon or decorative cord. Over her shoulders she wears a *chlamys* or small mantel, made from a rectangle of material about seven feet long and three and a half feet wide. It can be draped like the *himation* (see No. 30), or it can be worn in more casual fashion, wth one end hanging down the left side and the remainder passed diagonally across the back, under the right arm, diagonally up across the chest and flung back over the left shoulder. She holds a lyre made of wood or cardboard (see *Making Musical Instruments*, Pg. 68), and on her head wears a diadem made of Claycrete

(see *Making Jewelry*, Pg. 53.) The side of the chiton and
the hems of both garments are decorated with borders,
drawn with felt pen, made of appliqué, or actually em-

broidered, following classic designs, such as those in the
design panel that begins this chapter. In keeping with her
great beauty, Helen should be clad in the best draping
material available, such as light rayon, dacron or even silk.

30. SOCRATES

The Athenian orator and philosopher wears the orator's
cloak, the *himation*, worn alone, or as an outer garment,

over an Ionic chiton. Traditionally woven of wool, sometimes with a decorative border all around, the himation can be made from a rectangle of muslin or sheeting seven or eight feet long by the wearer's height, in width. To drape, as shown, hold one end under the wearer's left armpit, cross the material in front, under the right armpit and across the back diagonally to the left shoulder, as in a. Next, bring the material down over the left arm and turn it, b, as you cross the body. Draw it over the right arm like a sling and over the right shoulder, c. Cross back again and drape the final end over the left arm, d. The himation was worn as an outer garment by women as well as men (see No. 36). To make Socrates' white beard, see *Making Wigs and Beards*, Pg. 50. Now all you need for a pageant or play based on the siege of Troy is a giant wooden horse, or perhaps a silhouette cut-out to represent that legendary ruse.

31. NEBUCHADNEZZAR

The undergarment of the Assyrian tyrant is the basic sleeved tunic, or Hebrew and Persian *caftan*, later to become the Roman *tunica palmatica*. It is cut similar to the dress illustrated for Pocahontas, No. 25. The Assyrians often cut it up in front in an inverted V, to allow greater freedom for riding and hunting. Draper's fringe should be attached to its bottom hem. It is secured at the waist with a wide belt of leather or heavy cardboard, with a narrower belt over it.

The shawl is made of a rectangular piece of wool, muslin or linen, white, black, green or red in color. It should be about ninety by seventy-two inches for the average adult, and fringed on the two long sides. Fold it lengthwise to form a double tier of fringe, attach a length of cord to one

end at the fold. To drape, hold the cord at the waist, beginning at the right side, as shown, a. Now put all the material over the right shoulder, cross it at the back of the neck to the left shoulder, making a sling to hold the left arm, b. Bring the folded edge around the waist, passing the right elbow, b, then around the back and the left hip until about six inches in front of the left side of the waist, c and d. Fold the extra drapery underneath and confine the whole arrangement by a second cord, to which the first cord is tied, c and d. For convenience, shawls can be narrower and/or draped more simply. The method indicated, e, f, g, h, was usual for Assyrian women, but is also suitable for a number of other costumes of Biblical times. Nebuchadnezzar's beard and wig can be purchased, rented or made at home.

Making Beards and Wigs

A pair of clean cotton mops, dyed black and held in place with elastic can simulate the heavy strands of the Assyrian beard and hair, as shown, A. A fairly effective wig can be made of yarn, sewed in layers to a skullcap made from the top of a cotton or nylon stocking, B. Yarn or absorbent cotton (for Socrates' white beard) can be sewed or glued to a cambric or cotton beard foundation, with wire ear hooks, C. Beards and wigs can be made from other materials, such as crepe paper, raffia, string, and pieces of animal fur; or theatrical crepe hair can be applied directly to the face with spirit gum. (See the Make-up section of the author's 101 Masks for full details.) Fanciful wigs can be fashioned from just about any material, including paper, yarn, plastic, wood shavings, copper scouring pads. The elaborate wigs worn by Egyptian royalty can be made with a combination of colored yarns, gold cord and glass jewels, glued or sewed to a foundation of stiff cambric, cut as shown, D, glued or stapled into the shape, E, and

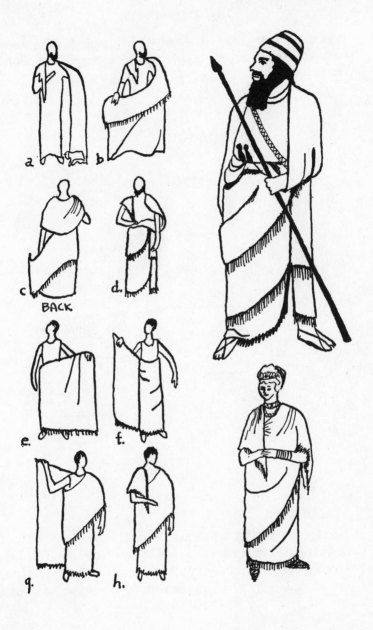

a

b

c

BACK

d

e

f

g

h

then decorated, either as a wig or a headdress. The same foundation can be used as the basis of a colorful headdress for Cleopatra.

A - MOPS

B

YARN

C

D

E

GLUE

32. CLEOPATRA

The Egyptian queen wears a full-length sewed chiton or basic tunic of white linen or cotton (see No. 7 and No. 29). It is secured high up under the breast with an embroidered or painted belt. She can also wear a thin wrap-around shawl. On her head she wears the vulture headdress, made of real feathers or of cardboard painted to look like feathers, B. Or she could wear the royal white plume, C. She wears jeweled bracelets and a be-jeweled collar, made of cardboard and cut as shown, A. Glass jewels and semi-precious stones can be fixed to the collar in settings of Claycrete.

Making Jewelry

Claycrete and molding mâché (see Papier-mâché, Pg. 42) make the best settings for glass jewels and semi-precious stones. Medallions, A, and other relief pieces can be built up on discs cut from heavy cardboard, thin wood or window

screening, and stones and glass can be pressed into the Clay-crete. Raised ornaments can be added to dagger and sword hilts, B; crowns, C; and bracelets, D. After jewels are fixed in place, the whole piece can be painted with gilt or colored paint and then shellacked. For permanence, mâché jewelry can even be electroplated. Glass and semi-precious stones can be picked up on the beach and polished in a lapidary's tumbler, or purchased already polished from any hobby or craft shop that carries lapidary supplies. Inexpensive settings for all kinds of costume jewelry can be purchased at the same craft shop. Bead stores are now plentiful in the larger cities, or you can consult your local hobby shop for bead and jewelry catalogues. Jewelry can be concocted from a great variety of odd hardware and made up in combinations from old costume jewelry itself. If colored glass is not available, try imbedding colored cellophane in Claycrete jewelry. Hard candy is nearly as effective, as are bits of broken bottle glass. For settings and relief, you can use plastic wood in place of papier-mâché.

33. PHARAOH

An early Pharaoh would have dressed as Cleopatra's younger brother is dressed here, in a figured cloak, which is really only a Semitic aba (see No. 13). Around his neck he wears a decorated collar (see No. 32). In his hands he holds the symbols of sovereignty and dominion, which can be made from cardboard or wood. His hat is the white crown of Lower Egypt, which will have to be molded of papier-mâché, built up on a tubular cardboard base. The red crown of Upper Egypt, E, would be less difficult to construct. Even less complicated is the royal wig-cover, F, which has a pattern of red lines, black yarn and gold cord, glued to the headdress foundation illustrated under *Making Beards and Wigs*, Pg. 50.

CLAY-CRETE

A

B C ↑

D ←

E

F

34. MARK ANTONY

Cleopatra's lover is dressed as an officer of the Roman Legion, wearing a metal *lorica* or solid breastplate. (See *Making Plate Armor*, Pg. 40.) With the addition of strap armor at waist and sleeves, the breastplate is worn over a plain chiton-tunic. His helmet is the more compact Roman modification of the Greek helmet. (See *Making Helmets*, Pg. 44.) As cape, he wears a simple *sagum* or *paludamentum*, a square of wool or heavy muslin, usually red, attached at the shoulder with a brooch, as shown. Or he can wear a longer, full-length cape, shown, I. When not in uniform, Mark Antony wore a *toga* in public, a *tunica* or sewed chiton at home.

35. CAESAR

All male Roman citizens in good standing were allowed to wear the *toga*. (Women wore the *palla*; see No. 36.) Roman emperors, such as Julius Caesar, wore the Imperial Toga, distinguished by its great size and its border of Tyrian purple, not "royal purple," but a rich plum or garnet color. This border ran across the upper edge of the toga, A, B, C and D, which was then folded down in preparation for draping, as shown, II. The material was usually cream-white wool and the garment was enormous: at least sixteen by six feet. The draping of the true Imperial Toga is very complicated and beyond the scope of this book, but instructions are included in more advanced costume books. (See *Historical Costumes*, Bibliography.) As with the palla, the Greek himation makes an acceptable and simpler substitute for the toga. (See No. 30.) Rather than wool, it can be made of unbleached muslin or medium weight sateen. On his head, Julius Caesar wore a wreath of laurel and bay leaves, called the "corona triumphalis." Later em-

perors wore similar wreaths of gold. Both can be simulated with real or plastic leaves affixed to a beret clip and left green or sprayed with gold paint. Romantic tradition has Julius Caesar as a contemporary of both Mark Antony and Cleopatra. The three historical figures appear in several popular plays and make excellent principle characters for a pageant or tableau.

36. MARY

As the principal character in the Christmas tableau, the mother of Jesus wears a full-length sewed chiton or plain tunic of muslin or rayon dyed light blue, overdraped with a himation (see No. 30) of darker blue, draped to cover her head. This overgarment is similar to the palla worn by Roman women. It can be up to four yards long by about fifty inches wide. To drape, pin one corner to the right shoulder, then draw diagonally across the throat, pulling part down upon the upper arm, part over the head to the right side, as in A. Bring it around the right shoulder, across the breast and over the left shoulder and arm, B. Then across the back and over the right shoulder, C. Finally, bring the end across the body, around the left hip (under the earlier fold), and around to the right hip, where it is held in the right hand. For a quicker and easier method, merely drape a wide blue shawl over the head, crossing the ends at the throat, allowing one end to fall down the breast, flinging the other back over a shoulder.

Staging a Tableau

Tableaux and pageants are alike in that there is seldom any dialogue spoken by the characters, although the story can be told by a narrator or chorus onstage or by an offstage voice, and music can be used to enhance the presentation. The pageant is more like a moving parade of characters and events;

A

BACK
B

C

the tableau is more like a fixed picture. If the characters move, it is only within the context of the picture, without entering or exiting. The usual Christmas tableau is presented with a movable screen or curtain, which opens to reveal the characters in place each time: Joseph and his wife entering Bethlehem; the Wise Men on their way to Bethlehem; the shepherds watching the star; the birth of the Babe; the Roman soldiers looking for Hebrew infants; etc. Costumes suitable for all characters, with variation and combination, have been discussed. Joseph and the shepherds wear Abraham's aba (No. 13). The Herald Angel can wear a long chiton or a loose, flowing aba of white rayon. One of the Wise Men can dress much like Nebuchadnezzar (No. 31). See also, Nos. 6, 7, 12, 27, 28, 30.

37. ROLAND

This bold knight of the Franks wears a full suit of chain armor under a Romanesque tunic or *bliaut,* which can be merely a sewed chiton with a wide skirt, cut after the pattern shown, with sleeves or without. It can have a high neck or be open, and is belted twice with cord or leather thongs crossing at the back. This costume is also suitable for King Arthur, Lancelot or Ivanhoe.

Making Chain Mail

Chain mail was made of linked metal, mesh, and metal scales. To reproduce the last, dye a set of long underwear gray and sew on discs of sheet metal, foil or gilded cardboard in overlapping rows. Mesh and linked chain mail can be made with linked or mesh metal pot scrapers sewed to long underwear or a close-fitting shirt and tights. It can also be fashioned from mop-cloth, which is coarse and woven into tubes suitable for covering legs, arms and neck. (The torso is covered by the tunic.) It can be dyed gray and tinted with silver paint. But the quickest and simplest method is to use garments of heavy

OR CUT ON DOTTED LINE

knitted wool—an old sweater for the torso, textured tights, ski socks or arms cut from an old sweater for the legs, a knitted ski hat or arctic face mask for the head. Dye them gray and give them a metallic look by brushing gilt paint across their surfaces.

38. SIEGFRIED

Of the same general historical period but of an opposing culture, this Teutonic hero wears a plain short tunic of rough muslin or burlap, laced at the neck; a wide belt of cardboard or leather, a cape of blanket material or artificial fur (see Special Fabrics, Pg. 92), and leggings of muslin held in place with criss-crossed garters of brown ribbon, elastic or adhesive tape. His helmet features animal horns, real or made from papier-mâché, built up on cardboard cones. This costume is also suitable for Scandinavian folk heroes, such as the great Viking mariner, Leif Ericson. His spear and battleax can be made from a variety of materials, as described below.

Making Battle Weapons

Most weapons in use up to the beginning of the twentieth century can be reproduced at the home workbench. (For later weapons, see *Making Firearms*, Pg. 126.) Spear shafts can be made from broom or mop handles, trimmed tree branches, bamboo or metal curtain rods. Some spear heads, like that of the barbed Samoan spear just below Roland's foot on Pg. 61, were actually made of hardwood. Heads like that of the medieval halberd (bottom of Pg. 61) can be jig-sawed or whittled from wood and gilded with metallic paint or wrapped with metal foil, or they can be cut from sheet metal. The Greek and Roman short sword, A, can be made from similar materials, with a wood or metal hilt guard added and the hilt itself wrapped with tape or metal wire, ribbon held in place by wire, or colored cord, glued in place and shellacked. Sword

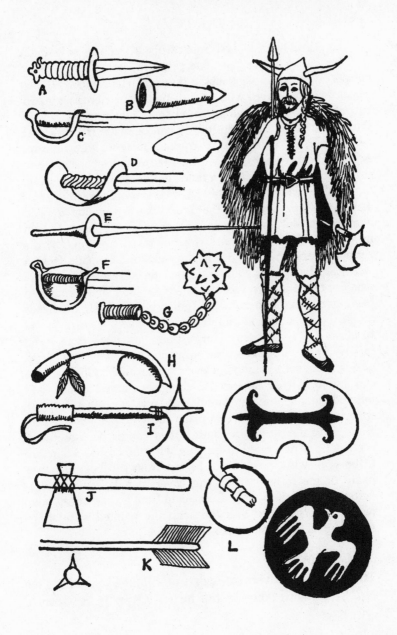

sheaths, B, can be fashioned from cardboard, canvas or leather, with leather or metal tips. The saber, C, is a military dress weapon with a simple knuckle guard of sheet metal. It becomes a pirate's sword with the substitution of a broader guard cut in the form of an ellipse from sheet metal or a large tin can, D. An elegant fencing foil, E, can be made from a metal curtain rod, with the handle wrapped in tape, wire or cord. A broad basket guard, F, can be cut from sheet metal, then either inscribed or cut with a fancy design. For actual fencing, the flexible blade of a real foil is necessary. Search the rummage and thrift shops and the dime store toy counter for odd hardware useful for weapons. The chain of the mace, G, can be purchased at a hardware store or taken from one of the various plastic toys. Its deadly business end is made from a styrofoam ball, with golf tees glued on all around, and the whole sprayed iron gray. A similar styrofoam globe is attached to a curved handle to make the Indian war club, H. The heads of the battleax, I, and the Indian tomahawk, J, can be cut from wood or sheet metal. The best bows are made from cured hickory or yew, but can also be made from other well dried woods, from split bamboo or even spring metal. Good arrows can be split from long cedar shingles, sanded round, and finished on the unpointed end with turkey feather fletches, split and trimmed, glued into place and wrapped with thread, K. Or, as in the case of the bow, arrows can be purchased and used as is, or decorated in keeping with the costume they are to be used with. Shields can be cut from cardboard, beaver board or metal, or garbage can covers can be suitably decorated. The small buckler, L, is made from a cane barrel hoop with canvas stretched over the hoop and painted, with straps to hold it to the arm, as shown.

39. CHARLEMAGNE

The Frankish sovereign wears a bliaut-like tunic (see No. 37) that reaches to the instep. Over it, he wears a

72"

surcote or *pelicon,* open at both sides, cut after the basic serape pattern shown. This outer robe has a yoke and lining of imitation fur (see *Special Fabrics,* Pg. 92). On his head he can wear a gentleman's fur-lined cap or a crown made of cardboard, covered with foil or gilded with paint and decorated with glass jewels in Claycrete settings (see *Making Jewelry,* Pg. 53). The pointed tips of his soft shoes can be reproduced by filling out the toes of tights or socks with cotton stuffing. (See *Converting Footgear,* Pg. 98.) This costume is suitable as the court dress of other kings and nobles of the Middle Ages, such as King Arthur and his knights, and Ivanhoe.

40. NORMAN LADY

She could be Charlemagne's queen or Roland's lady love. Over a long-sleeved tunic (No. 37) she wears a full-skirted bliaut with full, open sleeves, cut after the pattern shown. She is shown with her face discreetly framed by gorget and wimple—two large handkerchiefs, the first wrapped around the neck and pinned in back, the second draped over the head. But queens were privileged to wear their hair loose, and she might wear only a crown. This costume can serve for any of the elegant ladies of Medieval France, or for ladies of the Norman invasion of England in the late Middle Ages.

41. ROBIN HOOD

The legendary bandit of Sherwood Forest (center) wears the dress of the yeoman or free peasant farmer of twelfth through fourteenth century England. It can be made from whole cloth or from clothing on hand, elaborated with cut and sewed pieces. At its simplest, it is composed of a short basic tunic, dyed buckskin brown or Lincoln green, with

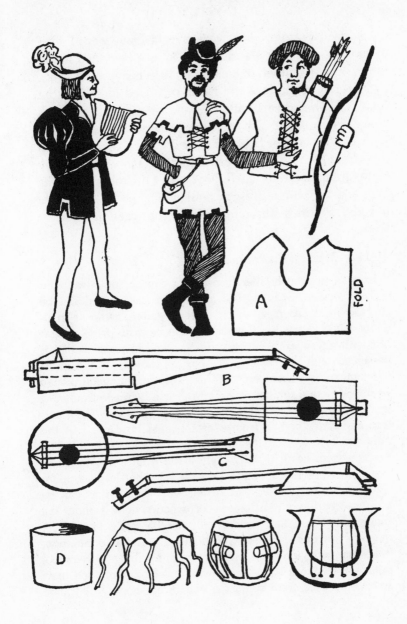

a scalloped bottom edge, worn over a long-sleeved shirt of contrasting color. A scalloped yoke can be added to the tunic. Brown or green tights terminate in heavy wool socks, padded out at the toes and rolled or folded loosely at the tops. A feathered cap, wide belt and shoulder-strap pouch complete the effect. The tunic can be laced across the front with tape or leather boot laces, or it can be replaced with a bolero, cut after the pattern shown, A, and worn here by Little John, standing on Robin's left. On Robin's right is Will Scarlet, whose dress is similar, but mostly in shades of red. He carries a harp made from construction board or wood.

Making Musical Instruments

Instruments can be merely props or can be "practical" and actually played. Stringed instruments are easiest and can be strung with inexpensive nylon or steel guitar, banjo or mandolin strings. A medieval mandolin can be made from a cigar box with a wooden neck, carved and glued in place so that it passes through the body of the box, as shown, B. A turn-of-the-century American banjo can be made from a metal piepan equipped with a similar neck, C. Frets can be made from cord wrapped around the neck and glued in place, following a pattern and order copied from a professional instrument of the same size. Bridge and pegs are carved from hardwood. The African drum has a tubular body made from a cookie tin or wooden detergent container, D, with a leather, canvas, inner tube rubber or plastic head strung with thongs that can be tightened with the insertion of short wooden dowels under the thongs. Cymbals, large and small, can be made from sheet metal or the tops of tin cans. With patience and determination, flutes can be made from metal or plastic tubing or bamboo, but most reed and brass instruments must be purchased, new as toys, or used from rummage and thrift shops.

See *Music and Dance*, Pg. 138, concerning the use of re-corded and live music in connection with costumes and dance. The small harp shown in the illustration can be jig-sawed from plywood and strung with nylon guitar strings.

42. KING JOHN

Norman tyrant of England and arch enemy of Robin Hood and his Merrie Men, John is shown here in a fur-lined cap and brocaded robe with full bliaut sleeves (see No. 40). Wearing equally dandyish dress is his cohort, the Sheriff of Nottingham, shown in flowered slippers, embroidered knee-length tunic and a large rectangular cape, secured at the shoulder with a jeweled brooch and printed with an elaborate design.

Printing Special Fabrics

Cheap modern fabrics come in a great variety of textures and designs, and many novelty fabrics can be purchased at reasonable prices (see *Special Fabrics*, Pg. 92). However, there may be occasions when the costumer will want to print his own special designs. Most craft and art supply stores carry fabric paints that can be brushed on by hand or used with stencils. For the design on the Sheriff's cape, stiff stencilling card can be cut with a razor blade, placed against the flattened fabric and brushed across with the desired color. Multiple color designs can be made with two or more stencils and colors. Designs can also be printed by linoleum block or even with potatoes, cut in half and incised with a design on the open face, then inked and used like rubber stamps to print the fabric. Silk screening, an elaborate process, can also be used for the printing of original decoration on most fabrics. For further decoration possibilities, see tie-dyeing, under *Dyeing Fabrics*, Pg. 70.

43. FRIAR TUCK

Robin Hood's good friend from the Church wears homely sandals and the coarse woolen habit of a Benedictine monk. His cloak can be made from heavy muslin, burlap, wool or blanketing. Cut as a giant-sized round cloak, A, with a hood added, B, it can serve as the dress of a common beggar, or, made of more impressive material, as the cloak of a gentleman or the vestment of a bishop, C. The friar's cloak should be dull rust, brown, or black, either natural or dyed.

Dyeing Fabrics

Packaged dyes are reliable and include directions for mixing and preparation of the dye-bath. If a considerable amount of fabric is to be dyed, it might pay to buy dye in bulk. Most dye manufacturers will send tiny sample packages or color samples on request. There are two kinds of aniline dye in common use. One kind is for vegetable fabric, mainly cotton. The other is for animal fabric, mainly silk and wool; but it will also dye hair, fur, feathers and skin.

The most common method is dip-dyeing—plunging the whole material into a dye-bath and boiling. Uneven effects, such as marbling, can be achieved by putting the material in wadded up and twisted. Patterns can be achieved, with experimentation, by either knotting the fabric before dipping, or tying off the desired parts with string, rope or strong ribbon. A pattern thus achieved with light dye of one color, can then be dyed a second color by dipping without tying.

Cheaper materials can be given a more expensive appearance through dyeing. Velvet can be simulated by uneven or spotty dyeing of flannelette or terry cloth. To simulate goat or camel's hair or other fur, dye flannelette dark brown, dark gray, wine red or dark yellow. While the material is still wet from the dye-bath, brush it the wrong way so that the nap is raised.

44. MAID MARIAN

Like her friend, Robin Hood, Marian preferred the dress of the common people of her time: a simple frock of green or brown, laced across the bodice, and a scalloped hood, A, cut after the pattern shown. Also shown, B, is a pattern for her laced bodice. The same hood is suitable for the jester of King John's court, who wears colorful tights and bracelets and anklets of strung sleigh or Morris bells, available in the stores around Christmas. Marian might also wear the more elegant dress of a court lady, including a long tunic or surcote, and *hennion* or pointed hat made of a cone of stiff white cambric and draped with a veil of chiffon or net.

45. KING RICHARD

Returned from the crusades to find Robin Hood still loyal, the lionhearted Saxon king is usually shown in chain mail and partial armor (see No. 28 and No. 37), but he could also wear a full set of plate armor, as shown here, the parts to be made of cambric and papier-mâché. (See *Making Plate Armor*, Pg. 40.) The breastplate is creased in the center and is laced at the sides to a flatter backplate. The *cuishes* and *greaves* (e and g) are held in place by loops of elastic or tapes tied behind thighs and legs. The *knee-cops* (f) are also held on with elastic loops and can be made from athletic knee protectors with cardboard "wings" attached. The *pauldrons* (a) are held to the shoulders by elastic loops that pass under the armpits. The *rerebraces* and *vambraces* (b and d) are slipped on like gauntlets, if tubular, or tied on, if half-plates. The *elbow cops* (c) can be made of small knee protectors. Gauntlets can be made from suitable garden gloves gilded with silver or black

A

B

FOLD

paint. The helmet can be made by the tab and glue process (see *Making Helmets,* Pg. 44) or it can be a wool ski hood, painted silver, with cardboard top and bottom visor plates, painted silver and attached to the cap over each ear. Shoes can be made of silver-painted heavy woolen socks with cotton-stuffed toes, slipped on over low street shoes. Or a separate foot plate can be made from cardboard. (See *Converting Footgear,* Pg. 98.) Similar armor can be worn by other medieval knights and jousting champions, such as Prince Valiant of the comic strips.

46. TOBY

Here is the classic rube of the chautauqua circuit and country tent show. He wears large, loose and baggy trousers of burlap or denim, cut after the basic trousers pattern shown. They can be secured around the waist with a piece of rope or held on with a single shoulder strap. Or he can wear an oversized pair of blue overalls, suitably worn and frayed. He wears a faded blue or red-checked shirt. A red-checked handkerchief is standard equipment for flamboyant blowing of the nose and other comic effects. Hanging out of a hole at the bottom of a back pocket, it looks like a wild red tail; pulled steadily out of the top of the pocket, it is a tail grotesquely withdrawing into the body. A patch or two can be sewed to the trousers, but don't overdo it. Toby wears huge clodhoppers without socks, and his face is liberally freckled. His nose can be rouged or he can wear a red rubber ball, hollowed out to fit the nose and held in place by elastic cord. Traditionally, Toby wears a carrot-colored fright wig, the hair of which can be made to stand on end with the tug of a concealed string. However, such wigs are hard to find these days and difficult to make. Instead, purchase an orange, red, or yellow rube wig, **or**

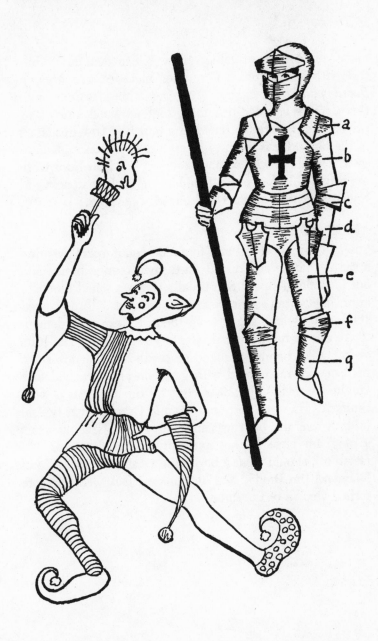

a

b

c

d

e

f

g

make your own by attaching crepe hair to a cambric skull-cap with spirit gum. (For other methods, see *Making Beards and Wigs,* Pg. 50.) Toby sometimes carries, some-times wears a broad-brimmed, high-crowned straw hat, frayed and battered, often with a bunch of cowslips stuck in the band. He is often to be seen chewing on a blade of grass or stalk of wild oat, and one or two of his front teeth are usually blacked out to give him the look of a backward but irrepressibly shrewd and cheerful hayseed.

47. ELLIE MAE

She is Toby's best gal and feminine counterpart, wearing a simple blouse and dirndl skirt, vivid orange braids and outsized clodhoppers. She usually wears a soiled gingham apron and often carries a tin bucket and a three-legged stool, upon which she is wont to sit, to rest or to demon-strate one of her principal talents, cow-milking. The brim of her poke bonnet is made of cardboard, cut after the pattern shown, covered with gingham and attached to a gingham crown. Other characters for the Toby plays wear similarly grotesque costumes. Pa and Granpa wear typical hillbilly overalls, big shoes and floppy hats. Granma wears a gingham poke bonnet and apron. The drummer, TB Hartburn, should wear a burlesque version of the attire of Diamond Jim Brady, No. 70. Banker Black wears a more formal version of the same.

5½"

SHOO, FLY, SHOO!

SHOO, FLY, SHOO!

A Toby Play, in One Act

Characters:

Toby	a rustic
Ellie Mae	his girl
Pa	his father
Granpa	his grandfather
TB Hartburn	a city slicker
Banker Black	a banker

and assorted hens, roosters, ducks, hound dogs, swine, and other livestock, as available, and including: Granma.

Setting: A hot, sleepy day in the Ozarks; the rickety front porch of the Toby family shack. Chickens and other animals wander about, or are heard offstage. A large wooden barrel stands to the right of stage center, the broad-brimmed black hat atop it indicating its human contents: Granpa.

A note on the production: *The Toby plays are basically farcical and can be played in free-wheeling, ad-lib style. Players need not stick strictly to the script, but may add lines or stage business as they see fit, with the emphasis on word play and visual humor. Much of the success of this particular sketch depends on contrast and interplay between the busy, con-*

descending bluster of the city slicker and the drawled, deadly
wile of the hayseeds, as step by step, the stranger finds himself
outflanked by his intended victims, and finally bamboozled
himself.

> The lights come up (or the curtain rises) to find Toby
> and Pa sprawled on the porch steps, head to head,
> their hats down over their faces. After a moment of
> silence, there is the loud buzzing of a fly, the sound
> of which is produced by the actor playing Toby. The
> fly appears to settle under his hat. He thrashes up-
> right, waving it away with his hat.

TOBY: Shoo, fly, shoo!

> The sound diminishes, the fly appears to go away. He
> nods his head in satisfaction, lies down again and puts
> his hat back over his face. After a moment of silence,
> the buzzing sound is heard again, this time made by
> the actor playing Pa. He thrashes upright, waving the
> fly away with his hat.

PA: Shoo, fly, shoo!

> The sound diminishes, the fly appears to go away. He
> nods in satisfaction, lies down and put his hat back
> over his face. After a moment of silence, the buzzing
> sounds again, this time from the barrel, stage right.
> The barrel begins to rock and the hat to hop on its
> top.

GRANPA: (from inside the barrel) Shoo, fly, shoo!

> The commotion increases, the barrel teeters, then the
> buzzing is cut off by a sharp SLAP! After a pause,
> the black hat rises, with Granpa's whiskered face
> underneath it.

GRANPA: (fiercely) When I say shoo, fly, I mean shoo! (He
produces an enormous papier-mâché fly, holds it a moment

like a trophy, then tosses it off right, and settles back into his barrel.)

> *Both Toby and Pa have revived enough to view this demonstration.*

TOBY: That was a big one, Pa.

PA: Sure was, Toby. But it's too late now, the dogs already got it.

> *There is the excited yapping of dogs offstage as he says it.*

TOBY: Well, they need the meat. (*He settles back down.*)

PA: (*Doing the same*) And the exercise.

> *A voluble muttering is heard, and Ellie Mae enters onto the porch from the house, a large, bedraggled dust mop thrust before her like a lance. As she babbles, she shakes the mop vigorously above the heads of the two men, emphasizing her points.*

ELLIE: Land'o Goshen, catchin' flies again, and me workin' my fingers to the bone marrow; three men in the house, and nary a one to chop wood or put the backhouse up straight; I swan, a body could fade away from the perpetual exhaustion and never be missed; it's work, work, work, day in, day out, and back in again . . . (*etc.*)

> *She gives the mop a last shake and, without pausing for a reply, turns and disappears back into the house, leaving behind a slowly settling cloud of dust and fluff. The two men have not moved.*

PA: (*after a moment, from beneath his hat*) That were your intended, Ellie Mae, weren't it?

TOBY: I believe it was, Pa. She sure is a fierce one for movin' dust around.

PA: Seems like it don't make much sense.

TOBY: Of course it don't, but it's the feminine thing to do.

PA: No, I mean it don't make sense to clean up a house that ain't yours no more.

TOBY: (*Straightening up a bit*) Lordy, I nearly forgot about that. Banker Black was comin' out to close the mortgage on us this week.

PA: I believe it were last week.

TOBY: Either way, he's late. By my calculations, it's already next week, beginnin' this mornin'.

PA: Well, he'll be along sooner or later, we can count on that. If there's anything a banker likes better than writing a mortgage, it's foreclosing on it.

TOBY: (*Settling back, blandly bitter*) Closing us out of house and home. (*Adjusting his hat over his eyes*) It riles me up.

PA: (*Unstirring*) I'm stirred to a powerful rage myself.

TOBY: I'm dangerous when I'm roused . . . (*His voice fades as he slips into slumber.*)

PA: (*Also falling asleep*) Dern tootin' . . . a reg'lar bearcat . . .

There is a long silence. Then a sudden commotion from the barrel, and another loud SLAP! Granpa's hat and head pop up from the barrel, and he gazes vaguely around.

GRANPA: I sure would like to go to town to see the movin' picture show, but the car's broke.

Without comment, he produces another giant fly, tosses it off right and sinks back into his barrel. There is the yapping of the dogs fighting over the morsel. Another silence. Then the sound of a motor car approaching offstage, left, and stopping. TB Hartburn enters briskly, carrying a large sample case.

TB: (*Effusively, in his carnival pitchman's sing-song style.*) Greetings, greetings, and what have we here? Why, it's the classic sylvan scene, the humble country cottage of homely but rustic grace, the gentle, patient natives, resting at the end of a day's honest labor. How peaceful, how touching, how . . .

Ellie Mae appears suddenly on the porch, babbling her endless complaint, blindly shaking her mop inches from the stranger's nose. The dust flies. There is a loud SLAP; Granpa pops up with another giant fly and throws it off right. The dogs yap, as Granpa settles back into the barrel. The dust and racket subside, to reveal Ellie Mae gaping at the stranger, and Toby and Pa with their hats tipped up, staring too.

TB: (*Brushing dust from his coat*) Yes, well, as I was saying, Greetings, Sirs, Madam or is it Mam'selle? (*He gives Ellie Mae his lady-killer smile. She giggles inanely, still gaping.*) Gentlemen, then. I appear to have lost my way. Perhaps you could tell me, how do I get to Shoo Fly Corners?

TOBY (*Deliberate and dry*) Don't move a step.

TB: Don't move a . . . (*he gets it*) Ah! Ha ha. Dry, rustic humor. I like that. Allow me to introduce myself. TB Hartburn, licensed domestic advisor and certified household consultant, at your service.

PA: What'd he say?

TOBY: Says he's a drummer.

TB: (*Opening his sample case*) Also, legal consultant, specialist in ailments of the alimentary tract, bones and liver, acclaimed clairvoyant, and reliable water douser.

PA: What'd he say?

TOBY: I believe he's tryin' to give the impression he's a religious man.

TB: (*Producing electric contraption from his case*) Now I happen to have here a working model of one of the greatest boons to the housewife since the double-ring ceremony. I refer to the Shovelux Little Demon Electric Carpet Sweeper and Vacuum Valet. (*As the words continue to flow, he attaches a hose to the machine, gathers up clouds of dirt and distributes them the length of the porch, and begins to unreel the appliance's electric cord. He is watched throughout with wry astonishment by the others.*) Now I couldn't help noticing the antiquated tool being used by the little lady here. Throw it away, young woman, stoop and strain no more. The Little Demon is here, replacing not only the back-breaking dust mop, but virtually every other old-fashioned household contrivance, while at the same time offering astounding ease of operation and a host of other labor saving devices. Through the wonder of electricity, the Little Demon will clean every nook and cranny of your house, will pick up anything from your carpet or floor, including the coarsest sort of earthen refuse, such as these clods. You ask for proof? Gladly. I spread the dirt, thusly. I guarantee you that the Little Demon will pick up every crumb from this porch. Should it fail in any way, I give you my pledge that I will, as they say, eat my words, and the clods of dirt also. (*He holds a clod in one hand, the plug end in the other. He notices the faint smile on Toby's face.*) You smile, my rustic friend. You doubt the veracity of my assertions.

TOBY: Not exactly, Stranger.

TB: Ah, then, Sir, is it that you have no faith?

TOBY: Nope. It's that we got no electricity.

> *TB's mouth drops open. He clears his throat painfully. He looks from the dirt clod in his left hand to the electric plug in his right, and back to the clod again.*

TB: No electricity. Ahem. Yes, I see, yes. Fancy that. Well, well. (*He drops both clod and plug briskly, brushes off his hands and changes his pitch.*) In that case, my dear newfound friends, you can count yourselves fortunate indeed, for I happen to have in my sample case here, the Little Demon Patented Hand Powered Carpet Sweeper ... (*He steps toward his sample case, but is brought up short by Ellie Mae's outthrust mop.*)

ELLIE (*Indicating the earth near TB's feet*) Watch out you don't get oil on them fancy gaiters, Stranger.

TB: (*Absently, stepping around the puddle of oil*) Oil, yes, strange place for it . . .

PA: Yep. Oozed out from under the porch there last week or so. Been meanin' to clean it up, ain't we, Toby?

TOBY: Sure enough. It started comin' outa them springs out back, and I reckon it just oozed on under the house and come out here. Sure does mess up the scenery, slicker'n bear grease too . . .

TB: (*He is rummaging in his sample case as this last soaks in and finally strikes home, driving him bolt upright, eyes starting.*) Under the house—springs—oil. Oil? Oil! (*He grasps the front of Toby's shirt in trembling hands.*) Oil? Did you say oil? Black gold? *Oil?*

ELLIE: If he said somethin' else, I didn't hear it.

PA: Easy there, Stranger, that gunk ain't no good for anything. Toby told you, it's from out back of the house . . .

> He stops short, hushed by a covert gesture from Toby, who is studying the Stranger closely. Toby winks at Pa and speaks, playing it dumb.

TOBY: Black gold? I don't rightly know what that means, Stranger.

TB: (*Struggling to get a grip on himself, trying to play it casually*) Why, of course you don't. Only an unreasonable man would expect a bunch of hicks . . . er, country people like yourselves to understand . . .

TOBY: Say, don't tell me that gunk is worth something.

TB: (*Hastily*) Oh no, not at all, worthless, gunk, indeed, worthless. Nothing like it to fatten your purse, er, flatten you worse. Terrible stuff, unhealthy too. Primary cause of the Black Plague. I'm surprised the county hasn't condemned your little home here.

TOBY: Wouldn't matter much if they did, we're thinkin' about moving, if we can sell the place.

ELLIE: Sell? But Toby, you know Banker Black is due to show up any minute to...

TOBY (*Cutting her off, furtively signaling her to shut up*) To make us an offer. Yes indeed, any minute now. Unless, of course, somebody gives us a better offer first.

ELLIE (*Getting it now*) A better offer... why shore, wouldn't that be nice.

PA: Dee-lightful.

GRANPA: (*Popping up from his barrel*) Dee-licious.

TB: Yes, well, perhaps I can help you.

TOBY: (*Stringing him along*) Help us, Stranger?

TB: Why, yes. Help you with your, uh, problem.

TOBY: Problem, Stranger?

TB: Why, with the house, selling the house.

TOBY: Oh, that's no problem. Like I said, Banker Black has made an offer, a mighty decent offer. Banker Black's a mighty decent fellow, for a banker...

TB: (*Suddenly out of control; hysterical with greed*) How much? How much did this banker offer? I'll top it! I'll double it! How much do you want? I'll drive to the city and go to my bank.

TOBY: 'Fraid there ain't time for that, Stranger, Banker Black is due any minute.

TB: But there must be a way, there has to be a way. How can I pay you, there must be a way!

TOBY: Well, now. (*Taking his time, he indicates off left to the others, then gives a questioning shrug of his shoulders. They comprehend and all nod their agreement. Toby turns back to the Stranger.*) Well sir, for a down payment, but only a down payment, mind you, we'll settle for that brand new motor car of yours over yonder.

TB: (*Relieved*) The car? Why of course, take it, it's yours. Now, I happen to have a blank deed with me, if you'll just sign here...

> *There follows a brief flurry of activity, during which Toby marks his X on the deed, Pa gets to his feet,*

and Ellie Mae ducks into the house and returns with
bundles of possessions, two of which she hands to
Pa and Toby. They all gather stage left, Toby facing
the Stranger, handing him the deed.

TOBY: Well then, there you are, Stranger, she's all yours. Hope that black gunk don't give you too much trouble.

TB: Oh, you needn't worry about that, I'll manage somehow. I'll just, oh, drain it off somewhere, put it in big barrels, you know, perhaps have a big steel tank made . . .

TOBY: Oh, I don't think you'll have to go to all that trouble.

TB: (*Uncomprehending*) Oh, it'll be no trouble, believe me.

TOBY: I mean, I don't think you'll be needin' any tank, or even any barrels, either.

TB: (*Uneasily*) No tank, no barrels? But how will I contain the stuff?

TOBY: Easy. Just let it soak into the ground.

TB: (*Aghast*) Soak into the ground?

TOBY: There ain't all that much of it, you see.

TB: (*Dawning horror*) Not all that much?

TOBY: Only that little bit that got to oozing out of the front seat springs of our old car out back. That much drained out of the crank case, but there can't be much more.

TB: (*Stunned, backing blindly to the porch steps, hands to his head.*) Front seat springs? Crank case oil? Old car?

TOBY: (*Cheerfully*) That's right, a 1918 Studebaker, and she's all yours.

TB: (*Delirious by now*) Front seat springs? Crank case oil? 1918 Studebaker?

Offstage, the car starts up. Toby is the last to back
offstage.

TOBY: An old car, but a good year. Consider her a trade in on your car. Mighty nice to have met you, Stranger. (*He exits*)

TB: Down payment. Front seat springs. Crank case oil. (*Releasing a deep groan, he collapses backward onto the steps.*)

GRANPA: Wait for me! (*He rises, barrel and all, and scuttles off left, toward sound of car.*)

> *At the sound of Granpa's exit, the Stranger revives slightly and tries to sit up, but he is immediately flattened by a little old lady exiting in a hurry from the house and scooting off left with a shriek and cackle.*

GRANMA: Wait for me, Toby, wait for your Granma!

TOBY: (*Offstage, left*) Granma, get aboard, get aboard!

> *The car engine roars, off left, moves away, fades. During the long silence that follows, the Stranger remains prostrate and motionless on the steps. Pa's hat, which has been left behind, covers the Stranger's face. Banker Black enters from stage right, carrying a briefcase.*

BLACK: (*To the world at large*) Greetings, greetings, what have we here? Why, it's the classic sylvan scene, the humble country cottage of homely but rustic grace, the gentle, patient native, resting at the end of his day's honest labor. (*The Stranger moves, lifts the hat and looks groggily up at the banker.*) My dear Sir, I appear to have lost my way. Perhaps you could tell me, how do I get to Shoo Fly Corners?

TB: (*Dully, wearily, after a very long pause*) Don't move a step.

BLACK: Don't worry about that. You see, I'm Judge Black, and I'm here to foreclose the mortgage on this place...

> *At this, the Stranger rolls quietly off the step like a log and remains dead still.*

BLACK: See here, what are you doing! Oh my stars, he appears to have passed out, poor fellow. Here now, Stranger, pull yourself together, you're getting crank case oil all over those lovely gaiters.

Curtain

48. QUEEN ELIZABETH

While this elaborate costume does require considerable work, it is not as difficult as it looks. A full, gathered skirt, made up or converted from an old evening gown, is divided in front to reveal the decorative petticoat underneath. The whole is supported underneath at the waist, by a farthingale, which can be made of wire, with a heavy cambric or leather waist band, A, of sheet metal, as a platform around the waist, B, or as a cloth bolster, stuffed with cotton and tied around the waist, as shown, C, and in cross-section, D. A bodice is made in two pieces, cut after the pattern given with costume No. 44. It is laced or attached with eye hooks down the front. Over this is fixed the pointed stomacher, E, a wedge-shaped panel of cardboard or buckram covered with material matching the rest of the bodice. A full-sleeved blouse with lace cuffs is worn under the bodice. Puffed sleeves can be "slashed" by simply tacking on double-pointed stripes of appropriate material. The standing ruff of starched lace can be held in place by an underpropper, made of wire bent and soldered as shown, F, and sewed to the back of the bodice to hold the ruff upright. It might be necessary also to sew a hoop of wire into the bottom hem of the skirt to help it hold its shape. Elizabethan ladies also wore the fluted ruff. (See No. 49.) This costume is also suitable for other ladies of the seventeenth and eighteenth centuries, including Mary Queen of Scots and Catherine de Medici; as well as for a fairytale queen, Cinderella at the ball, and several of Shakespeare's ladies. Both men and women of the Elizabethan age wore plenty of jewelry. Sumptuous materials were popular, especially brocades, with lavish addition of braid and lace wherever possible.

Special Fabrics

To imitate heavy materials, many rich and some with high luster, search the upholstery departments for fabrics such as rayon brocades and damasks. Heavy figured flannelette, sold for bathrobes and towels, looks elegant on the stage, as does figured terry cloth. The rayon satins and taffetas sold for coat linings are sumptuous from a distance, as are the heavier sateens. A great variety of cheap novelty fabrics are available at theatrical and store display supply houses, including such exotic materials as silver and gold lamé, tapa cloth and other materials made from vegetable fibers, fluorescent fabrics, imitation fur of all kinds, zebra stripe and leopard spot cottons, as well as such useful trimming as inexpensive braid, beading, lacework, sequins, feathers.

49. SIR WALTER RALEIGH

Sir Walter's formal court clothes are much like those which Capt. John Smith wears under his armor. (See No. 24.) The full sleeves of his blouse and the puffed legs of his short breeches can be given their slashed appearance as with Elizabeth's sleeves (No. 48). His doublet, worn over the shirt, is really only a short sewed tunic (No. 12) or basic shirt (No. 26), with sleeves removed and the garment decorated with strips of brocade or braid. For wrist lace, buy cheap, coarse torchon which shows up well on stage, but must be starched; or some of the new nylon lace. His cape can be short (No. 21), or long (No. 34), and should be lined for elegance. His hat can be made of velveteen or converted from a large beret or wide-brimmed fedora by addition of a white ostrich plume or cockade made of fluffy chicken feathers. He wears tights and heelless slippers, which can be elaborately decorated. The white ruff can be made from starched gauze, muslin, lace

organdy, nylon or rayon net, or even crepe paper. But tarlatan is easiest to work with. Make a neckband of white
belting three inches wide, A. For a ruff three inches wide
and four to six inches deep, you will need a strip of tarlatan
thirteen inches wide and about three yards long. Cut it
crosswise, not on the bias. A deeper ruff will require a
longer strip. Double the strip to make it about six inches
wide, then fold it, fanlike, into six inch accordion pleats, B.
Arrange the pleated strip around the neckband and pin
the apex of the pleats to the top edge of the band at regular
intervals. Turn the whole thing over and whipstitch the
pleats to the reverse edge of the band, then turn again and
stitch again. To open the pleats into smooth S-curves, run
a curling iron or heated rod inside each sharp edge, damp-
ening the tarlatan slightly first. For a fancier effect,
starched lace can be sewed to the folded outside edge of
the strip before pleating, or gold or silver paint can be
dabbed on the outside edge. Hooks and eyes hold the neckband in place at the rear. The ruff can be curl-ironed back
into shape after each wearing, but it cannot be laundered
and can be dry-cleaned no more than once. Sir Walter's
costume is suitable, with variations, for Sir Francis Drake,
Henry VIII (a), William Shakespeare (b), Charles I and
James I of England, Richelieu and Francis I of France,
many Italian and Spanish noblemen and explorers of the
period, such as Christopher Columbus, Ponce de Leon,
Balboa, Pizarro, and Cortez; or for poor, deluded old Don
Quixote; or for a fairy-tale prince or king (c).

50. SPANISH LADY

She wears the ruff and stomacher worn by Queen Elizabeth, but her skirts are supported underneath by a bell-
shaped farthingale much like the wire contrivance used to

6"

3½"

HEAD SIZE

give a hoop skirt its shape (see No. 64). Wearing the high
comb draped with the black lace shawl or *mantilla* (pro-
file), she could be any Spanish gentlewoman from the sixteenth century up to present times, when such elegant
dress is still worn on festive occasions. Her black fan can
be made from folded paper, suitably decorated, or from
lace, starched after folding.

51. SPANISH BULL FIGHTER

This is the *traje de luz* or "suit of light" worn by such
storied matadors as Manolete and El Cordobes. The tailored jacket and knee-breeches should be of the same color,
with contrasting decoration—white or pale green with gold
embroidery, pale or dark blue with silver, beige or pale
blue with black. Embroidery can be done with braid and
rickrack, or can be more elaborate and include sequins,
tassels or small mirrors or jewels. Oval epaulets are cut
from cardboard or stiff cambric, covered with matching
fabric and embroidery, finished with tassels and attached
to the shoulders. A stiff white shirt front can be made from
cardboard or cambric, with studs inserted or painted on,
and a black string tie added.

The traditional hat or *tricornio,* can be made from the
crown of a black fedora, with two round balls about 2½
inches in diameter covered with a nappy matching fabric
such as terry cloth and sewed into place over each ear. At
the back of the hat, or to the nape of the neck, attach a
black, fabric-covered button with a curled tuft of black
hair: the pigtail or *coleta,* official badge of the matador. A
red sash can be added. Knee-breeches can be made from
old trousers or cut and sewed in a narrowed version of the
basic trousers pattern, using some silken material such as

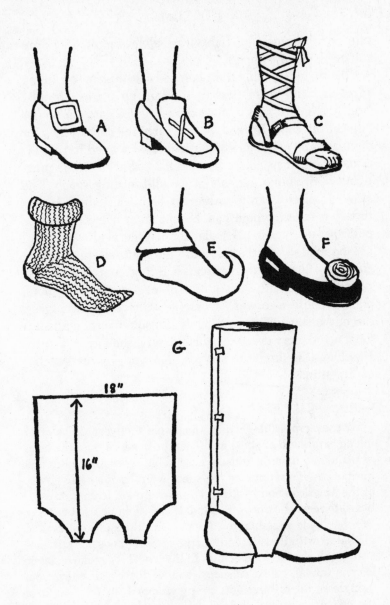

A

B

C

D

E

F

G

18"

16"

sateen. Stockings (use tights) are always pink. Shoes are soft-soled ballet slippers.

This matador holds the plain red felt *muleta*, or killing cape, in position for passing the bull by a cross, formed from the sword and a short dowel sewed into the upper edge of the cape. Instead, he can carry the *capota*, a larger circular cape (see No. 43) of yellow satin lined in red. He is also shown here in the less formal garb worn while practicing with young animals at a bull-breeding ranch. The sleeved bolero is gray, as are the high-waisted, wide-bottomed trousers, which can be cut from a basic trousers pattern (see No. 46). His flat-topped hat is also gray and can be made with the tab and glue method (see *Making Hats*, Pg. 28). He wears Spanish riding boots, which can be reproduced with the addition of leggings to street shoes, and he might also wear spurs (see *Converting Footgear*, directly below). This costume is also suitable for a Spanish flamenco dancer or any Spanish dandy, such as Don Juan. In white, it is similar to the costume worn by the gauchos of Argentina.

Converting Footgear

Whenever possible, convert available footwear. Buckles of gilded cardboard or sheet metal can be fastened over the laces of plain-toed oxfords to make acceptable shoes for pirates and puritans, A. To reproduce the shoes worn by the early gentry of the American South, attach large tongues of leather or cardboard to regular oxfords, B. Sandals can often be used as is, or can be made suitable for Greek and Roman soldiers and gladiators with the addition of criss-crossed thongs or tapes, or with black elastic, which clings to the leg, C. To make a classic Roman sandal, called *calcaeus*, remove the elastic sides from "congress gaiters" and add straps wrapped up the length of the calf. Heavy wool socks can be extended with padding to

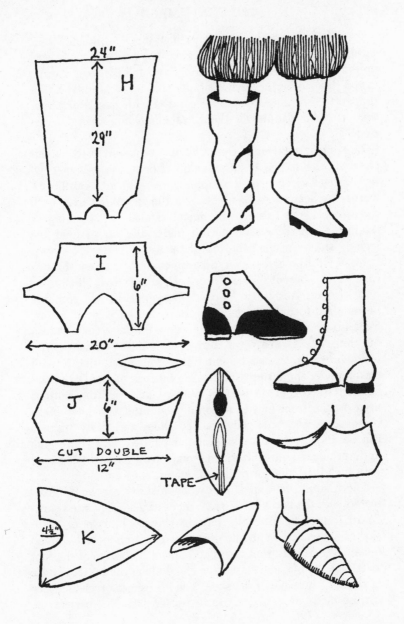

24"

H

29"

I

6"

20"

J

6"

CUT DOUBLE
12"

TAPE

4½"

K

make slippers or soft boots with pointed toes, D. Stiffened with cardboard inner soles and Claycrete, they can be made to curl up for an Arabian Nights effect, E. Such a "sock shoe" can be sewed to a rubber or leather slipper sole for durability. Ballet slippers or low shoes can be decorated with tassels or imitation roses for dandies of the Elizabethan and Georgian periods, F.

Leggings can be made from a variety of materials to convert street shoes into just about any kind of boot. For gaiters, cowboy or jack boots, cut a simple shape, G, from cardboard, leather or heavy vinyl and fit it to the lower leg over each shoe, securing it behind with metal catches or by gluing or sewing. Loops of elastic passed under the instep hold the legging snugly against the top of the shoe. The wide-topped boots of Elizabethan soldier, Spanish conquistador and French cavalier can be cut in the pattern, H, from vinyl, oil-cloth or heavy canvas. Additional loops of elastic, inside, will probably be required to hold the legging above the knee; or it can be folded over and allowed to hang below the knee for a swash-buckling effect. Spats for turn-of-the-century dandies and vaudeville hoofers can be cut from similar material, I, with elastic under the instep and the side buttons painted or sewed on. Extend the ankle portion upward and put the buttons more to the front and in a double row, and you have high-buttoned lady's shoes. High-heeled shoes and party slippers can be decorated with pom-poms or painted with white glue and sprinkled with glitter; and plain oxfords can be gilded with metallic paint for theatrical effect.

The unique shape of Dutch wooden shoes can be approximated with the addition to street shoes of yellow-painted cardboard spats, cut after the pattern shown, J. Two of these shapes should be bent into shape over the shoe and stapled down the rear and front edges and down the bridge of the foot as far as possible, and stapled or glued along the bottom edges of the heel and sole of the shoe. The iron shoes of plate armor can be made of gilded cardboard after a similar pattern, K,

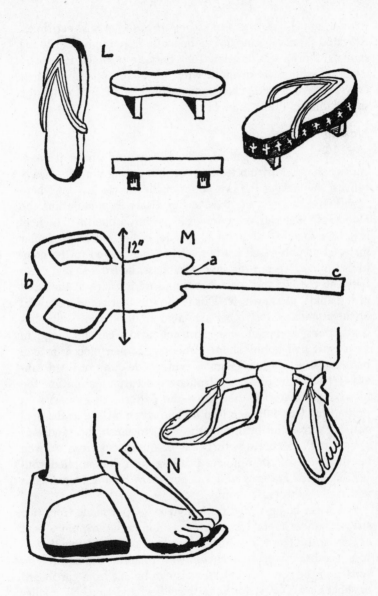

L

M

12"

a

b

c

N

folded, tunnel-like, and also stapled in place over street shoes. Elevated Japanese sandals can be made from the rubber thong sandals sold for beach wear. Tack them to plywood risers and decorate with paint or finish with brocaded upholstery fabric or velveteen, sewed, glued and stapled in place around the sandal and on the thongs, L.

Making Footgear

To make a simple sandal, from the ground up, as it were, cut the shape, M, from leather, soft but strong vinyl, or heavy canvas, shellacking the raw edges of the canvas, except where it will pass between the toes, a. For a sure fit, first outline the foot on the material, then draw the pattern around it. The heel is sewed together at point b. A sole, either cut from similar material or purchased ready-made, is then sewed to the completed upper. To put the sandal on, pass the front thong, c, up between the big and second toes and tie in place at the front of the ankle, as shown, N. This is the *solea*, or common sandal of the Romans. Most other sandals require special skills, but instructions, materials and construction kits can be found in most craft and hobby shops. American Indian moccasins can be made from leather, chamois skin, suede cloth or dyed canvas. To make the one-piece Iroquois moccasin, first outline the foot on the material, then draw the pattern, O, around it in proportion. Cut out, then fold up and stitch or lace at the heel and up across the bridge of the foot, to finish the sandal as shown at P. Decorate with beads or quills, cut from chicken feathers or dyed, or simulate beading with dots applied with felt ink pens. Patterns and kits for more complex moccasins are available in craft shops.

Spurs can be jig-sawed from plywood, Q, or made from two strips of sheet metal, strap iron or aluminum stripping, bent as shown, R. The two pieces are riveted or bolted together to form the basic horseshoe shape, with room on the end for insertion of the round rowel. Rowels can be cut from cardboard or sheet metal; larger for Spanish soldiers and gauchos, smaller

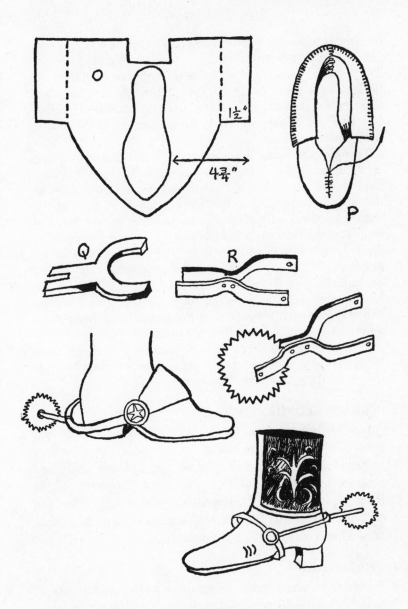

O

1½"

4¾"

P

Q

R

for American cowboys. Bits of metal can also be attached and allowed to dangle at the heel for that cowboy jingle-jangle. The Spanish spur has a broad strap of leather or vinyl over the bridge of the foot, tied or buckled at the inside of the boot, with a silver shell-like disc or concho on the outside. The cowboy spur has a narrower strap. Both spurs require a second strap or loop of elastic running under the instep.

To make the giant clown shoes for Emmett Kelly's tramp clown, first cut two "soles" from quarter-inch plywood, S, then rivet or nail (nails driven downwards) a pair of old shoes to the wooden soles, butting the heels of the shoes back at the narrow end of each plywood sole. Leather, canvas or vinyl overshoes are then cut, after the pattern, T, and decorated as desired, including eyelets for laces. The overshoes are sewed at toe and heel, then placed over the actual shoes and tacked or stapled under the edge of the wooden sole. To cover the bent-over ends of nails and provide traction, glue a rubber half sole onto each plywood sole. For wearing, the inner shoes must be laced tightly first, then the overshoe. With practice, a dedicated clown can learn to lean precariously forward with his big brogans as braces, to the point where it seems he must fall on his putty nose, yet does not.

52. TRAMP CLOWN

Any old baggy coat and trousers will do, with one knee and one elbow out and patches discreetly placed. He wears a battered derby or crumpled fedora, a thatch wig, and a red nose modeled with nose putty, made of papier-mâché, or from a ping-pong or hollowed-out rubber ball. (See the author's *101 Masks* for make-up details for this and other clown faces. See No. 51 for clown shoes.)

53. HARLEQUIN

He wears a short tunic or tailored jerkin, and tights of matching pattern, usually of varicolored triangular patches,

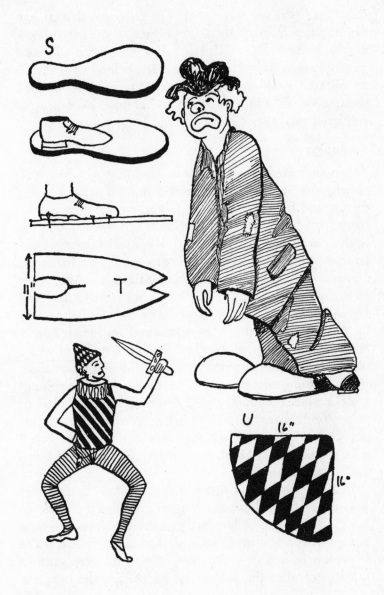

sometimes polka-dotted or striped. His cone-shaped hat can be made from cardboard, buckram or soft felt, following the pattern shown, U. His half-mask can be cut from black paper or dyed buckram, secured behind with elastic or ribbon. Traditionally, he wears a rabbit's-foot and wooden sword at his belt and goes barefoot. He can wear a colored ruff. (See No. 49.)

54. PIERROT

This is the grandfather of the modern Whiteface and Joey clowns, who are usually costumed similarly (smaller figures, a and b). Pierrot's loose jacket and trousers can be made from basic patterns (see No. 26 and No. 46), or from slightly oversized pajamas, with pom-poms of bunched and trimmed yarn, crepe paper or cotton, ranged up the front. He wears matching pom-poms on his shoes and hat, which is similar to Harlequin's, but with a soft turned-up brim. He wears a simple neck ruff, cut after the circular pattern in the center of the illustration and gathered into a flounced collar. He can also have gathered ruffles of gauze or matching material at wrists and ankles, and wears clean white cotton gardening gloves. Or he can wear the voluminous one-piece costume (small figure a), cut from plain or cotton print, after the pattern in the bottom left-hand corner. Or he can wear the tailored brocade jacket and broad satin pantaloons of his elegant modern European descendant (small figure c).

Pierrette, the girl of Pierrot's dreams, sometimes wears the ruff and conical hat, and is usually costumed in a simple bodice, tights and ballet skirt, or tutu, which can be pure white or decorated with polka dots to match her hat. The sleeveless bodice or waist should be made from satin or sateen, cut after the pattern shown, A. For the tutu, cut

a

b

c

A

four rectangles of tarlatan or rayon or nylon net, gather each into petticoat folds with a saddle stitch, then lay the four skirts one over the other and sew them to the waist, with both top and skirt opening at the back, to be secured with hooks and eyes.

55. CAVALIER

This dashing gentleman-soldier of mid-seventeenth century France or England wears a "buff jerkin" of canvas or muslin, dyed to imitate leather. Convert an old coat, or cut and sew, following one of the basic tunic patterns. (See No. 37.) Leave the tunic open at the front, or secure it loosely with braid loops or frogs. Sleeves can be decorated with horizontal braiding, as shown, or the jerkin can be worn sleeveless over a cotton or linen fencing shirt or woman's blouse with leg-o-mutton sleeves. A similar effect can be achieved by covering a full-sleeved shirt with a sleevless open-sided tunic made after the basic serape pattern (see No. 39), cut shorter and wider and decorated with a gold cross of Lorraine or other musketeer insignia, as in small figure, a. The scabbard sash is made of broad ribbon, or can be cut from upholstery material or made of canvas, with decoration drawn on with felt pen. The hat should have a low crown, a soft, broad brim, and be decorated with an ostrich plume or some substitute, such as a bundle of turkey feathers. The wide-topped hip boots are allowed to fold down upon themselves, rather than being folded over and outwards. (See *Converting Footgear*, Pg. 98.) At court, English and French cavaliers wore similar but more elaborate dress (smaller figure, b), often with lace collar and cuffs, and bunched ribbon on the hat. The gentleman shown wears a large, dark-colored "disguise cape" (see No. 43 for pattern). This costume is suitable for

the Three Musketeers, or for Rostand's large-nosed poet-hero, Cyrano de Bergerac.

56. LOUIS XIV

Fifty years after the Musketeers, the French king and his gentlemen wore shoulder-length wigs (see *Making Beards and Wigs*, Pg. 50), longer coats and more elaborate finery. A flared woman's coat can be converted with the addition of braid frogs, loose, full shirt cuffs, and a cravat or lace handkerchief tied at the throat. The narrow knee breeches are made from a basic trousers pattern, cut narrow and gathered below the knee with elastic. Stockings are white tights. This costume is also suitable for Louis XV, Louis XVI, Charles I of England, and other dandies of the seventeenth and eighteenth centuries.

57. MARIE ANTOINETTE

Louis XVI's queen is reported to have remarked, when told that the poor had run out of bread: "Then let them eat cake." She is shown here got up something like a wedding cake herself, in the exaggerated style of the late eighteenth century French court. The towering wig is further heightened by the addition of plumes; the waist is made to seem narrower with a wedge-shaped stomacher (see No. 48); the hips are made massive by enormous skirts, supported underneath by wire panniers, A, and puffed out by the addition of yards of satin ribbon and gold braid. The costume is nearly as impossible to make as it was to wear, but a reasonable imitation can be put together, using either a bustle or a hoop skirt arrangement (see No. 64), instead of the cumbersome panniers. Such a costume would be equally suitable as the court dress of Madame du Barry and Catherine the Great; for characters in such plays as

A

a   b   c

She Stoops to Conquer and *The School for Scandal;* for the "Dresden" shepherdess; or for one of the better-dressed Fairy Godmothers.

58. JOSEPHINE

The first French Empire marked a return to simpler neo-classic lines in women's dress. Napoleon's lady friend is shown (a) in a typical high-waisted gown with short puffed sleeves and a long, straight skirt, which can be reproduced by converting suitable modern apparel. Lace and ribbon were used discreetly. The back of the popular Watteau gown of the period was cut full and stitched in two double box pleats, as shown (b). Simplified versions of the Empire dress were worn in early nineteenth century England and America, often with elbow-length gloves and poke bonnets (c) sometimes held on by chin ribbons. Such costumes, with but slight variation, are suitable for female characters from Dickens' *David Copperfield;* and for characters in *Vanity Fair* and *Pride and Prejudice.* The similar dress worn by the child is known as a Kate Greenaway and is suitable as the costume of any early American child, such as Becky Thatcher, Tom Sawyer's friend. To costume Tom, try a tidied-up version of No. 46. Don't bother to tidy up for his pal, Huck Finn.

59. BEAU BRUMMELL

French, English and well-to-do American gentlemen of the Empire Period wore square-tailed cutaway coats which could be buttoned up high in front or worn open, with the wide lapels folded back and a starched linen stock at the neck. Trousers were worn tight and to the ankle, or knee breeches were worn with boots. Wool was the popular fabric; colors were dark green, blue, mustard yellow, buff and

A

B

black. Convert an old dress coat or use one of the commercial costume patterns for the coat; they are available usually in children's sizes. Make the high crowned beaver hat by the tab and glue method (see *Making Hats*, Pg. 28), or add a high crown to a hard-brimmed fedora, as shown, A. The costume is suitable for a Dickens' character such as Mister Micawber, and for America's friend, Lafayette.

60. WELLINGTON

Uniforms of the Napoleonic wars followed civilian fashion, modified with wide sashes and braided coat fronts. For the epaulets, cut horseshoe shapes from cardboard, B, decorate with gold braid and fringe or yarn brushed with gold paint, and attach to shoulders. The cocked officer's hat is made from a very wide-brimmed felt hat or sombrero, with the brim turned up at front and back and pinned to either side of the crown. A sword sash of wide ribbon can be draped from the shoulder across the body instead of wrapped around the waist. Such a uniform is suitable for Napoleon as well as for his English antagonist, Wellington, who can also wear the high black boots named for him. (See *Converting Footgear*, Pg. 98.)

61. GEORGE WASHINGTON

Gentlemen of colonial America wore clothes similar to those worn by their European counterparts of the same period. (See No. 56, No. 59, No. 60.) Favorite colors for the frock coat were black, blue, brown, green and plum. It was usually made of wool, but sometimes of silk or satin. The ruffled neck stock was made of fine linen, but can be reproduced in muslin or cotton. A waistcoat can be made of upholstery brocade, or a man's vest can be substituted. To make the three-cornered hat, pin up the brim of a flat-

topped felt hat on three sides, or, if possible, reblock it. For the knee breeches, adapt a basic trousers pattern or tuck regular trousers into high stockings. For buckled shoes, see *Converting Footgear*, Pg. 98. To make the powdered and ribboned periwig, consult *Making Beards and Wigs*, Pg. 50. This costume is suitable for such founding fathers as Benjamin Franklin and Thomas Jefferson, for Nathan Hale, Paul Revere, Lafayette, George II and George III of England, Monsieur Beaucaire, and Louis XV.

62. REVOLUTIONARY SOLDIER

British and American soldiers of the late eighteenth century wore similar uniforms, the British usually red, the American blue or brown. Lapels are long and squared, made of coarse wool, burlap or velveteen and decorated with frogs of braid. White cross-belts are similar to those worn by school-crossing guards and can be made of heavy muslin or canvas. Add round plastic or wooden buttons up the sides of tight black or white canvas leggings. The drum is made from a detergent bin (see *Making Musical Instruments*, Pg. 68), and decorated with an eagle decal, available at hardware stores. A powder horn and bullet pouch can be made of papier-mâché. For the saber, see *Making Battle Weapons*, Pg. 62. For a flintlock musket, see *Making Firearms*, Pg. 126. The minutemen wore less formal versions of this uniform at the Battle of Bunker Hill.

63. RHETT BUTLER

A similar frock coat was worn by gentlemen of the deep South just before and during the Civil War. The broad lapels of the Empire Period had narrowed, and the trousers were looser, but still narrow at the bottom. Waistcoat, narrow beaver hat, and black string tie complete the costume of Scarlett O'Hara's great love, as well as that of many a riverboat gambler, and of such frontier dandies as Bat Masterson, who replaced the beaver hat with a derby.

64. MARTHA WASHINGTON

Full skirts, supported by petticoats and/or hoops, were the formal dress of American ladies throughout the eighteenth century and well into the twentieth. Wigs were worn only by women of fashion. The basic full-skirted dress can be reproduced by converting an evening gown, combining full skirts and a suitable blouse, or following one of the commercial patterns available. America's first First Lady is shown here in a full skirt of silk, sateen or rayon brocade, split to reveal her petticoat. The bell-like shape of the dress is maintained by the hoop skirt construction underneath, A. To a waistband of heavy muslin or other belting, attach ten or more muslin tapes in a radial pattern. Make four wire hoops. For a grown woman, they should be about 1¼, 2, 2½ and 3 feet in diameter. Arrange them one above the other in a tier and suspend them from the vertically hanging tapes. The skirts can be worn loose over this framework, or it can be sewed permanently into the dress. A similar effect can be achieved without the hoops by draping fabric bolsters at the hips, as illustrated for the second colonial dress, B. To imitate silk and satin, use mercerized poplin, rayon or lightweight cambric. Either costume is also suitable for Molly Pitcher and for such colonial ladies as Betsy Ross.

65. FRONTIER GAL

Shown here carrying a water bucket, the woman of the frontier wore similar but much simpler dresses, most often without hoops. Decorate cotton print or poplin with modest trimming of lace or rickrack. A full apron should be added. For the poke bonnet, make a modified or cut-down version of that illustrated with costume No. 47.

66. SCARLETT O'HARA

The tempestuous heroine of *Gone with the Wind* wore full hoop skirts and a long-sleeved jacket for afternoon wear, more elegant bodices of ruffles and lace for evening wear. As with No. 64, above, a more modest version can be put together without hoops, of cotton or poplin, with simpler ruffles above the elbows and over the hem of the overskirt. A small boater hat often carried a plume or ribbon. Southern belles often carried fans to ward off the "skeeters" and keep the sun off their flawless complexions. Such a costume is also suitable for Civil War ladies of the North, such as Mary Todd Lincoln.

A

B

67. ULYSSES S. GRANT

Officers in the Union and Confederate armies dressed very much alike, the one in federal blue, the other in medium gray. Frock coats were belted with fringed sashes, red or yellow-gold. Hats were broad-brimmed and flat-crowned, with cords and tassels. Shoulder boards can be made from fabric-covered cardboard, with insignia painted on or made with braid, A. Imitation brass and silver buttons of plastic are available, or wooden buttons can be wrapped in foil. For boots, see *Converting Footgear*, Pg. 98. This uniform, in gray, is equally suitable for Stonewall Jackson or General Robert E. Lee, of the Confederacy. For several decades after the Civil War, U.S. Cavalry officers wore a modified version of the same uniform, blue, with yellow cording on the hat, yellow neck scarf, white or yellow gauntlets, and a broad yellow stripe down the side of the pants. The foolhardy "General" George Custer wore such a uniform, as did other renowned Indian fighters of the late nineteenth century.

68. JOHNNY REB

Union and Confederate enlisted men also wore similar uniforms of blue or gray. The jacket can be made from an old suit jacket with the lapels turned up and imitation brass buttons added. Cover a round candy box with canvas or muslin to make the canteen. The hat can be made from the bill and base of an old billed hat, with collapsible cloth crown and cardboard top added; or it can be made up from three pieces cut from cardboard and glued together by the tab and glue method, as shown, B. The long musket has a bayonet and can be made at the home workbench. (See *Making Firearms*, Pg. 126.)

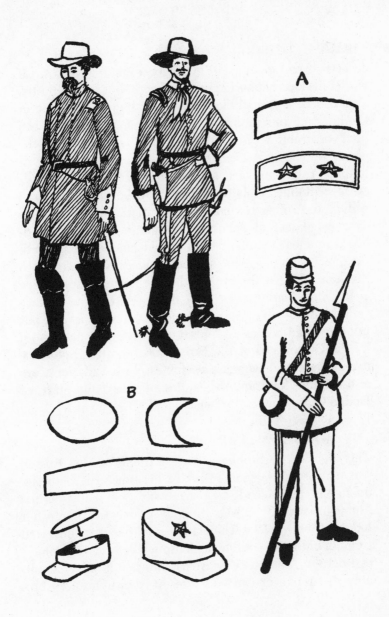

A

B

69. LILLIAN RUSSELL

As actress and glamor girl of her time, the late 1800s, Lil wore full skirts supported, not by hoops, but by the bustle. This can be a stuffed cloth bolster resting on the back of the hips and tied around the waist, as shown, A, or it can be a construction of coiled wire, also suspended from the waist, B. The gown can be decorated with a variety of draping, ruffles and lace, and hats of most previous periods are acceptable. A plain umbrella can be decorated with ribbon and ruffles to make the chic parasol. She can also carry eyeglasses-on-a-stick, or a lorgnette, made from cardboard or sheet metal, or from an old pair of glasses with the temples removed and a handle added. Hidden beneath the hem of her skirt are her high buttoned shoes. (See *Converting Footgear*, Pg. 98.) By the end of the century (still Miss Russell's time), the bustle had disappeared, but full skirts had not, as evidenced by the elegant dress worn by the Gibson girl of the early 1900s (bottom right corner). These two women's costumes, with variations, are also suitable for frontier beauties such as Belle Starr, of Dodge City fame, and others.

70. DIAMOND JIM BRADY

This high living gambler and close friend of Miss Russell was one of the fashion plates of his time. His high silk opera hat can be made by the tab and glue method. (See *Making Hats*, Pg. 28.) Or it can be converted from a felt fedora. (See No. 59.) The claw-hammer coat is converted from an old dress coat or made up whole after a commercial pattern. The fancy waistcoat can be an old vest suitably decorated, or can be made up from upholstery bro-

cade, following the bolero pattern (see No. 41). A heavy watch chain of gold-gilt plastic or brass hardware chain is looped across his belly. Trousers can be black or striped. Spats are worn over black shoes or gaiters (see *Converting Footgear*, Pg. 98). His walking stick can be made from a broomstick, enameled black and bound with brass wire or striping, or from suitable metal tubing. Mold its "ivory" head from Claycrete, or search the hardware counters for an ornate drawer-pull or other piece of hardware. Diamond Jim sometimes wore a derby, and his costume can be worn with a flat straw hat. Clothing like this, with variations, was worn well into the twentieth century, and is also suitable for such "robber barons" as J. P. Morgan, as well as for actors, dandies, gamblers, politicians and such.

71. DAN'L BOONE

He wears fringed buckskins (see No. 26) and moccasins (see *Making Footgear*, Pg. 102), and carries a flintrock musket (see *Making Firearms*, directly below). His coonskin hat can be made of artificial fur (see *Special Fabrics*, Pg. 92), or from strips cut from an old fur coat found in the attic or at a thrift shop. Wrap the fur around a skullcap cut from an old felt hat, then attach a real raccoon tail or a strip of fur sewed in a long roll and trimmed with scissors. Build the shape of the powder horn with Claycrete on a cardboard cone, adding a shoulder strap and ornate plastic top from a cosmetics jar. A bullet pouch can be made of leather or can be a decorative perfume or other bottle, fitted with a leather neck and thong. Like the buckskins, the knife sheath is made from leather, chamois skin, vinyl, canvas or oilcloth (see *Making Battle Weapons*, Pg.

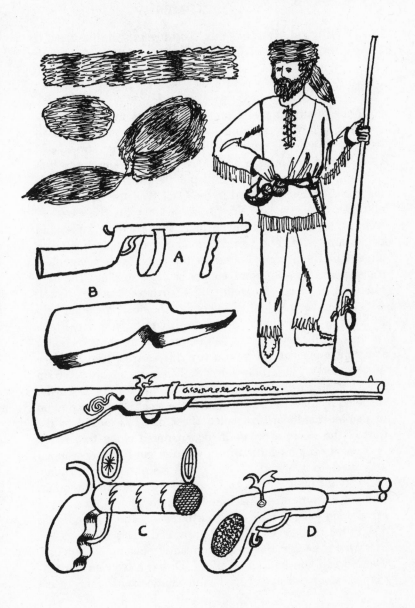

A

B

C

D

62). With modifications, this costume is suitable for Kit Carson, Buffalo Bill, Wild Bill Hickock, and Davy Crockett.

Making Firearms

Of the great variety of imitation firearms available at toy counters, a few are useable as is and many can be made to look more authentic with the addition of shoulder straps, odd hardware or a little paint judiciously applied. Some prop firearms may have to be made by hand. To make a muzzle-loading musket of the sort used in the Civil War and by frontiersmen like Dan'l Boone (No. 71, above), jig-saw the stock, B, from a piece of 2x4 13 inches long, shape with a knife, and paper, and stain. The barrel is made from half inch pipe or aluminum tubing and bound to the stock with silver electrician's tape, or aluminum, copper or brass striping. The long ramrod is a piece of curtain rod or painted wooden dowel, with one end seated in the front end of the stock, the other held in place at the business end of the barrel by additional tape or striping. A trigger guard can be made from sheet metal, or the trigger mechanism from a toy rifle can be fixed in place on the stock. The ornate flintlock hammer can be cut from sheet metal, cardboard or heavy aluminum foil, or it can be modeled in Claycrete, then fixed to the stock. Final decoration of painted cardboard or tooled sheet metal is tacked to the butt of the stock, and inscribed or painted along the barrel. A bayonet can be whittled from wood or cut from sheet metal and fixed to the end of the barrel with tape or striping. Other types of firearms can be made from similar materials. The old Thompson submachine or Tommy gun, A, favorite of Prohibition gangsters, is cut from boxwood and finished with a short tubing barrel, real pistol grips, and a circular magazine jig-sawed from ¾ inch plywood or made from a movie film can. The old cap and ball pirate pistol, D, has a wooden banana-shaped stock, tubing barrel and flintlock hammer. Most modern firearms, from the cowboy's Colt 45 onward, are available in authentic reproductions. Weapons of the future can be made from just about any hardware available. The "ion disintegrator" shown, C, is made from a toilet tissue tube, camera hand grip and an assortment of drain filters. It is best never to use operating firearms at masquerades or on the stage. If they are used, they must be checked before and after use, by at least two persons, to make sure they are not loaded. And even then, statistics prove, you are taking a serious life-and-death risk.

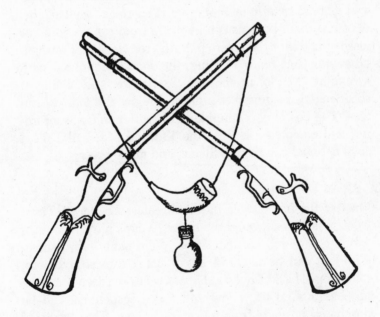

72. THE VIRGINIAN

The better-known items of cowboy apparel are easy to come by, but some articles will probably have to be made. The sheepskin chaps shown here can be reproduced by first making "batwing" chaps, A, of denim or canvas, then covering them with dyed toweling or artificial fur (see *Dyeing Fabrics*, Pg. 70, and *Special Fabrics*, Pg. 92). Plain batwing chaps are made of leather, canvas, or soft vinyl, cut after the pattern shown, B, and decorated with round "conchos" cut from foil, cardboard or sheet metal. "Shotgun" chaps are tight leather or vinyl leggings (see No. 26). A vest without buttons can be made from canvas, vinyl or leather, cut after the bolero pattern (see No. 41). For regular roping and fancy twirling, the rope is equipped with a running "hondo" at one end, C, with an inside lining of sheet metal, to give it weight and allow the loop to run free. The costume is suitable, with variation, for such renowned cowpokes as Billy the Kid and Marshall Dillon, such fictional cowboys as Shane, and many others.

73. PAUL BUNYAN

Most of the items worn by the Greatest Logger of Them All can be found around the house. Wear a navy blue wool watch cap or red knitted ski hat. "Tin pants" with stovepipe legs can be made of heavy black canvas or denim, following a basic trousers shape. Or "Frisco jeans" can be purchased. Red or yellow and green suspenders can be purchased or made from muslin or belting. The sleeves of Paul's long johns protrude from under the rolled-up sleeves of his checkered shirt, and can be the sleeves of a red sweater worn underneath. A quick corncob pipe can be

ANKLE TO CROTCH

A

B

C

made from a piece of dowel and a chunk of corncob. Ax and peavey, the principal tools of Paul's trade, have wooden shafts and hardware jig-sawed from plywood, or cut from heavy cardboard and built up with Claycrete. The peculiar construction of the peavey head, designed to grip logs so they can be rolled and manipulated, is shown in the bottom right-hand corner of the illustration. This costume, with variations, can also be used for such hard-working folk figures as Mike Fink, riverboat man, Joe Magarac, steelman, and John Henry, who beat that steam drill down.

74. ZAPATA

This Mexican *bandido* wears the plain shirt and trousers of the Mexican peasant, reproduced with loose pajamas or made of white cotton or unbleached muslin cut after basic shirt and trousers patterns (see No. 26). His enormous sombrero will have to be purchased, although he can wear a cowboy hat or the flat Spanish hat (see No. 51). He might also wear the traditional serape (see No. 39), either plain white or rainbow colored. The *bandoleras* or ammunition belts crossing his chest can be made from three-inch-wide bands of leather, canvas or vinyl, with narrower strips forming the bullet loops and sewed, stapled or riveted in place, A. Although they terrorized the Texans along the Rio Grande, such men as Zapata, Juan Cortina and Pancho Villa were heroes to their people, and still are to this day. The white shirt and pants, together with the serape, are worn by many of the native peoples of South America, with variations in hats and decoration. Combined with the flat hat, a wide belt and boots instead of sandals,

A

B

this outfit represents the dress of the cowboy or gaucho of Argentina.

75. RED CLOUD

As shown here, the chief of the Oglala Sioux fits the popular picture of the American Indian chief. For his fringed buckskins, see No. 26. For moccasins, see *Making Footgear*, Pg. 102. The red stone war pipe can be made from painted doweling, or from Claycrete, and decorated with chicken or turkey feathers. The bone chest decoration can be reproduced by stringing colored soda straws and mounting them on a cotton or chamois bib. To make the full feathered headdress, first make a close-fitting skullcap from buckram or cut it from the crown of an old felt hat. You will need at least two dozen large chicken or turkey feathers and half as many smaller feathers. Trim the upper end of each to a point and dip in dark brown or black ink, to simulate eagle feathers. Next, prepare each feather by cutting the quill end at an angle, then bending it around upon itself and binding it in place to make a loop, as shown, B. Sew about half the feathers upright around the cap, the tallest at center-front, diminishing in size around to the back. Next, cut a "tail" or strip of buckram or red or black felt about three inches wide, and attach the remainder of the feathers to it, loop stitching a heavy thread from one to the other up the full length of the tail, to hold the feathers at right angle to it. Attach the tail to the rear of the cap, C. Add a one-inch band of buckram or suede across the forehead, decorated with felt point pens or with real beading. Finally, add small, fluffy feathers to the base of each large quill, and two tufts of small feathers as "sideburns," hanging in front of each ear. Each large feather can be

finished with the addition of three or four short lengths of colored yarn or darning silk, glued to its tip.

Also shown, are four of the many thousands of different costumes worn by the once more than 144 distinct American Indian tribes. Sitting Bull, also of the Sioux, and primarily a spiritual leader, is shown here in medicine man garb. His buffalo headdress can be made from an old fur fixed to a skullcap, the horns made from papier-mâché or Claycrete. In one hand he holds eagle-bone whistles; in the other, he holds a tortoise-shell rattle, which can also be made of Claycrete. The Hopi kachina dancer beside him wears a simple skirt and cape of cotton or muslin, decorated with sewed bands of crepe paper, and a kachina mask, made from an oatmeal box, a length of toilet tissue tube, and feathers; and painted with poster colors. (For full details on this mask, see the author's *101 Masks.*) The fringes on his legs are cut from crepe paper and held in place with elastic.

The Navajo hoop dancer wears a head roach, which can be made from a strip of coarse fur, such as coyote or wolf, curved over the center line of the head and held in place with chin straps. It might also be made from crepe paper (see *Making Helmets,* Pg. 44). The hoops, which he steps through and passes up his body as he dances, can be made of wire or green branches or cardboard and decorated with crepe paper or feathers. Or he could dance with rattlesnakes, made of stuffed and painted tubes of jersey; tickling them with a feathered stick to distract them.

Finally, Crazy Horse, the great Sioux warrior and martyr, is shown stripped for action, wearing little more than his personal war paint, "given" to him in a dream: white

hailstones on a black and red background, with streaks of yellow lightning across his face. (See *Body Paint,* Pg. 178.)

76. GREEK DANCER

The traditional man's costume of Greece is called the *fustanella,* and is still worn by dancers on festive occasions. The short, fluffy skirt can be made of permanently pleated white nylon crepe or of three or four layers of crepe paper, one over the other. White tights are decorated with tasseled ribbons just below the knees. Convert soft slippers with red yarn pom-poms. A red sash at the waist supports the knife in his broad sheath (see *Making Battle Weapons,*

Pg. 62). A woman's blouse makes a good substitute for the full-sleeved white shirt. The scarlet vest is fastened on the right-hand side with a row of twelve red, blue or silver buttons; and can be cut after the basic bolero pattern (see No. 41), altered to have a high neck and rounded collar. With the finishing touch of a long stocking cap, preferably red with a blue silk tassel, the costumer is ready to dance with Zorba the Greek himself.

77. HIGHLAND DANCER

The Greeks are not the only men to wear skirts as part of their traditional garb, and they certainly are not the only ones with a lively national dance. The girl shown here is

doing the Highland Fling over two crossed swords, while wearing a man's pleated wool kilt cut from whole cloth or from an old plaid blanket. (Underneath, wear dark-colored swimming trunks. Yes, they are traditional.) Hanging on a metal chain from the broad leather belt is the *sporan*, a silver mounted purse made of sheep's wool. To imitate, convert an old silver chatelaine bag or other purse by adding crowded tassels of white yarn and finishing with two long tassels of black in the center. Wear wool stockings of matching plaid or plain color, and brown or black brogans. The sport coat is dark green, blue, brown or black, and as short as possible. Over the left shoulder, drape a folded tartan shawl and secure it with a large ornamental brooch or clasp. Top off the costume with a real tam-o'-shanter or make one from a beret by adding pom-pom and ribbons; or wear a military hat made by sewing a plaid band to an army overseas cap.

Music and Dance

Costumes, music and dancing are often combined for folk festivals, square dances and other social occasions. A folk costume masquerade party can be enlivened with recorded music from the various countries represented in costume. Folk dances performed by authentically costumed performers are a welcome addition to amateur variety shows, and modern dance exhibitions can be enhanced by imaginative costumes. Keep an ear out for recorded music that might be useful for future masquerades or costume performances. Dressed in authentic costume, Zorba the Greek might dance to the soundtrack LP from the film of the same name. Folkways Records of New York City has an excellent catalogue of folk music.

Research

Folk costume varies infinitely in detail, not only from country to country, but from region to region and tribe to tribe, and even from town to town and village to village. Where the strictest authenticity is desired, further research will usually be necessary. In the cases of the more complex and difficult costumes, further investigation will also be necessary into materials and methods. Consult the bibliography at the back of this book for basic volumes. Your librarian can be a great help, both in guiding you to books on the library shelves, and in directing you to other sources.

78. DUTCH MAN AND WOMAN

Like most Old World countries, Holland boasts dozens of folk costumes, similar in general, but different in detail. Shown here is a man of Marken on the Zuyder Zee. His full, dark gray breeches come just below the knee. His jacket, also gray, can be converted from a tight-fitting, double-breasted coat, with silver buttons added. In the summer, he wears a felt hat with the brim turned up, in the winter a close-fitting fur cap. His shoes are wooden sabots (see *Converting Footgear*, Pg. 98), but he could wear soft black leather slippers, like the woman of Volendam, beside him. She wears the full skirts of most European peasant women, with the special decoration shown. Her hat is made of starched muslin lace or organdy, with "wings" cut as shown, A, with a single dart on each to give it its cupped curl; the two wings attached on either side of a skullcap of similar material. Similar winged hats, sometimes reenforced with wire, are a part of Swedish, Danish and Flemish folk dress.

79. MANDARIN AND WIFE

This is the costume of the well-to-do gentry, government officials and scholars of Old China. The design of the em-

broidered square on the man's chest represents his station
and branch of service: a bird for the civil service, a wild
animal for the military. His hat can be made from an old
felt hat with the brim cut down and turned up, a button
added on top, and a long feather or strip of bright embroidery hanging down the back. Coat and skirts can be made
up of upholstery brocade or converted from a woman's
embroidered housecoat and evening skirt, many of which
are made up in pseudo-oriental design. The mandarin's
wife wears equally gorgeous and highly embroidered
skirts and a long cloak, with full sleeves of nylon net or
chiffon. Confucius was a scholar and mandarin; the in-
famous Fu Manchu wore a similar costume. The clothing
of the common people of China was much simpler, consist-
ing mainly of pajama-like blouse and trousers (see No. 5).
The basic pattern for a coolie hat is shown, B. It can be
made from cardboard, with straw matting glued on the
outside.

80. MAN AND WOMAN OF INDIA

The man is shown in the high-necked Nehru jacket, fast
becoming the popular dress of India. It can be made of
cotton, muslin or brocade. His trousers, of similar material,
narrow at the ankles. He can wear a turban (see No. 81,
below), or the cotton cap shown, similar to an army overseas cap or those worn by fry cooks. The woman wears the
sari. It is about six yards long and about forty inches wide,
of cotton, silk or both, embroidered or printed. It is worn
over a short white shirt or blouse called a *choli*, and a petticoat tied around the waist by a drawstring. One end of the
sari is folded into small pleats and tucked into the petticoat
drawstring, then wrapped around to form a skirt. The remainder is carried up in front and flung over the left shoulder. The end is then left to hang or is brought around in

A

18"

4"

B

front and draped over the arm, or over the head as a hood. The sari is worn by Hindu women. Moslem women sometimes wear trousers like those worn by the man.

81. SULTAN AND HAREM GIRL

The lavish garb of the Turkish and Persian sovereigns and the Indian and other maharajahs of the past century varied greatly. A generalized version like that shown can be got together out of whatever luxurious garments and accessories are available, including brocade dressing gowns, silk pajamas and costume jewelry. For his pointed, turned-up shoes, see *Converting Footgear*, Pg. 98. A turban can be sewed permanently in place on a skullcap or around a *fez*, shaped like a flower pot and made by the tab and glue method (see *Making Hats*, Pg. 28). The harem girl is shown here in a bathing suit halter and nylon net bloomers over a bathing suit bottom. She might also wear an embroidered and be-jeweled bolero (see No. 41). She wears lots of bracelets and bells on her ankles. She may wear jewels in nostril and navel and rings on fingers and toes. Her veil is of nylon net. A caste mark of ruby red make-up rests in the center of her forehead.

82. GEISHA

The traditional basic garment of Japanese women and men is the kimono, A, front; B, back. It is a difficult garment to make from scratch, but kimono-like garments are available as bath and casual wear. The kimono of the Japanese gentlewoman is usually of a subdued hue, with a very bright lining. Geishas and actresses, on the other hand, usually wear bright, garish kimonos, with subdued linings. The *obi*, or sash, is almost always gaily colored, and is four to six yards in length and from twelve to fifteen inches wide. To put it on, fold it lengthwise, turning the two edges

upward. Wind it twice around the waist and tie the two
ends at the back, either in a butterfly bow, for unmarried
women and brides, or in the flat, squarish knot shown, B.
This knot can be duplicated by simply folding the ends
into a box shape and stitching in place, or the box knot
can be made detachable from the sash. Short white socks
are worn with thonged sandals (see *Converting Footgear*,
Pg. 98). The kimono of the Japanese man is sometimes
worn shorter (judo robes can be substituted). He wears
a narrower sash, called a *heko-obi*. Over his kimono he
sometimes wears a black silk, wide-sleeved, knee-length
coat. He can go bareheaded or wear a straw coolie hat
(see No. 80). Both men and women carry Japanese bamboo umbrellas when out of doors.

83. AFRICAN MAN AND WOMAN

The men of Nigeria and many parts of Africa wear a kind
of aba, made much like the Mexican serape (see No. 39),
with trousers underneath. These large tunics are most often
of gaily patterned cottons and are often richly embroidered
at the neck. On his head, the African often wears a tie-
dyed turban, or he can wear a maroon felt *fez*, as shown.
African women often wear exotic prints also. A woman
from Liberia wears a bodice top of brightly flowered print,
gathered at the waist. She wears a shawl of another fabric.
Still another colored print forms her large gathered skirt.
She too wears a loose turban. The tribes of Africa are very
numerous, and their costumes differ from locality to locality. The Masai woman of Kenya, shown here, wears her
hair cropped close. Large metal hoops are at her ears,
neck, arms and ankles (make them from aluminum, brass
or copper wire). Her cotton or woolen wraps are loose and
large, of dark maroon, brown or blue. She is shown here
with a painted gourd hanging from her shoulder.

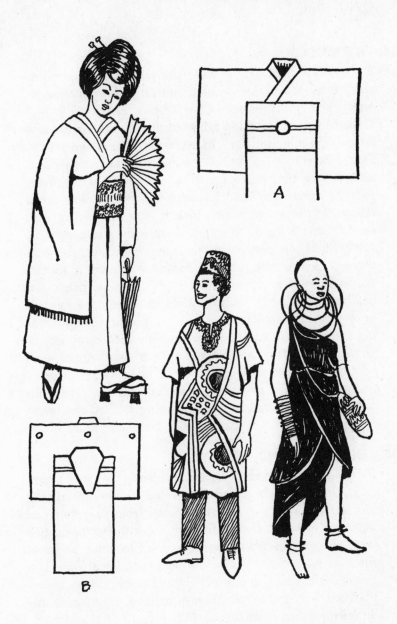

A

B

84. ASTRONAUT

Use nylon or denim coveralls. If they are not an appropriate "space" color (electric blue, liferaft yellow, fluorescent pink), you can dye them. (See *Dyeing Fabrics*, Pg. 70.) Make tubing of matching fabric, stuff with cotton and sew on as fat piping at collar, elbows, wrists, knees and ankles. Paint heavy shoes or ski boots a matching color of enamel and, if possible, build up soles and heels with silver-painted wood. Run insulated wire of various colors down the outside seams of arms and legs, threading it through sewed loops or taping it in place with silver camera tape, available at photography stores. Or you can run the wire through clear plastic tubing. Use silvered rubber industrial gloves or garden gloves sprayed with metallic paint. For headgear, use a toy "bubble" helmet, or equip a football or motorcycle helmet with a full-face plastic visor, attaching a shoe polish can or other simulated intercom microphone inside. The "life-support system" is mounted on a hiking packboard and composed of whatever electronics and other odd hardware and household throwaways available, such as old vacuum cleaner tubing, quilted aluminum foil, plastic strawberry boxes, old transistor radio cases.

85. OLD YEAR AND NEW YEAR

Father Time wears the long Ionic chiton (see No. 7), sandals, a long white beard, and a printed ribbon proclaiming him the Old Year. Model his hourglass from Claycrete and paint it; or make a frame of wood, break the stems off two wine glasses, tape them together, point to point, and seat them in the frame. His sickle has a handle of dowel or broomstick, and a blade of silvered construction board, plywood wrapped in foil, or sheet metal. Cupid wears only an outsized diaper or breechcloth (see No. 6), and a rib-

bon naming him the New Year. He can wear small wings of foil or silvered cardboard on his bare heels or on sandals, and he carries a small bow and quiver of arrows.

86. SANTA CLAUS

From the pom-pom tip of his red stocking cap to the heels of his converted black street shoes, he is costumed in apparel and accessories already described in this book. For the fur trim of hat and coat, see *Dyeing Fabrics*, Pg. 70. For the beard, see *Making Beards and Wigs*, Pg. 50. Make the suit from pajamas, red or dyed red (see *Dyeing Fabrics*, Pg. 70). Make the broad belt from leather, vinyl or painted cardboard. He wears white dress or white cotton garden gloves. To reproduce his shiny black boots, consult *Converting Footgear*, Pg. 98.

87. SATAN

To raise the devil in a hurry, fashion a scarlet hood (see No. 44), and add papier-mâché horns (see *papier-mâché*, Pg. 42). His blouse is a tight red jersey sweater, and he can wear a bolero (see No. 41), of black, trimmed in red, or vice versa. He wears red tights or long underwear dyed scarlet (see *Dyeing Fabrics*, Pg. 70). His toes can be merely pointed, or they can be turned up. (See *Converting Footgear*, Pg. 98), or he can wear low black boots, converting from street shoes with the addition of vinyl leggings. His cape can be black and lined in red, or vice versa; it can be oval (No. 34), short and circular (No. 21), or long and circular (No. 43). Cut the tines of his pitchfork from plywood and wrap in foil or gild, or cut from sheet metal. Provide him with a brimstone atmosphere by dropping dry ice in a bucket of water concealed somewhere nearby.

Design

Costume design is like any other art in that there are really no hard and fast rules. There are, however, certain basic principles, which must first be understood before they can be flaunted effectively. The purpose of this brief chapter is to outline those principles, then to offer suggestions for exploiting, bending and breaking them, so that the individual imagination might be freed to have its say.

Line, Pattern, Color

Taken alone, a costume can be judged by certain basic qualities: line, pattern, and color. Line refers to the "shape" of the costume—the configuration and silhouette-outline. Pattern refers to the arrangement of the various elements within that outline, including the pattern and texture of the materials used. Color refers to the color combinations employed, as well as the overall color effect, or "tone." Color basics are not as complicated as they might at first seem to be, and are vitally important to good design.

The Color Wheel

For full understanding of color, you need to study briefly a color wheel. Various kinds are available at art supply stores; one is diagrammed here in black and white, with the colors labeled by name.

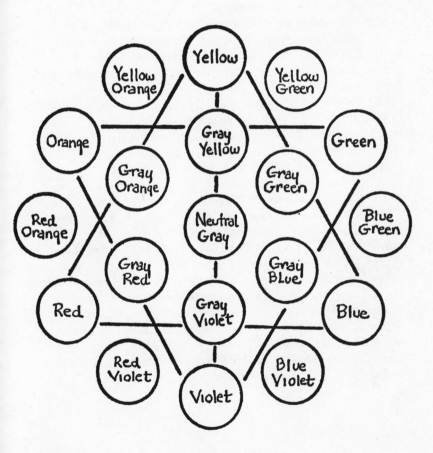

Various of the colors on the wheel are related to one another in certain ways. There are primary colors, analogous colors, binary colors, complementary colors. Certain of these relationships between colors can be "dialed" with the use of the "needles" shown on the two smaller color wheels.

No dial is needed to locate the three primary colors: yellow, blue, and red. They are at the points of the upright triangle within the wheel. They are called primary because they are not produced by mixing other colors, whereas all the other colors on the wheel are mixed.

Any color made by mixing two primary colors is called a binary color. Mix red and blue and you get the binary color, violet. Blue and yellow make green. Red and yellow make orange. These three binary colors are located at the points of the inverted triangle.

Mix a primary color and a binary color, and you get an intermediate color, such as yellow-green, blue-green, blue-violet, and so on. Each intermediate color is next to its nearest cousin on the wheel. Not shown are the infinite number of gradations between neighboring intermediate colors.

As everyone has noticed, some colors seem soft or warm, some seem hard or cool. With yellow at the top of the color wheel, a line can be drawn vertically down the center. The colors at the left of the line are known as the warm colors. The colors at the right are considered to be cool. Red is warm, blue is cool, yellow is in-between.

The so-called complementary colors form a balance of warmth and coolness. Any two complementary colors can be located by attaching a double arrow to the wheel, with its center on neutral gray. Place one point of this arrow on a color, and that color's complementary color, or "complement," will be at the opposite point of the arrow. For instance: red-violet, and its complement, yellow-green.

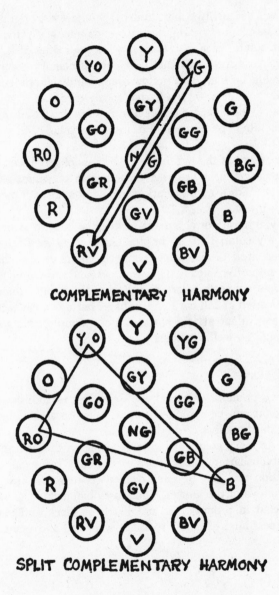

COMPLEMENTARY HARMONY

SPLIT COMPLEMENTARY HARMONY

To "dial" not just two, but three harmoniously related colors, use a three-pointed, triangular arrow, matching a primary or an intermediate color with the colors on both sides of its complement. An example of this split complementary color harmony would be blue with yellow-orange and red-orange. The three colors go more or less harmoniously together.

Analogous or adjacent colors are those which lie next to or near each other on the wheel. For instance: yellow and yellow-orange.

Value describes the lightness or darkness of any given color (not shown on the wheel). A combination of values can be harmonious. For example: dark green combined with medium and light green.

Finally, intensity or chroma describes the brightness or dullness of any color; that is, the amount of gray mixed into it. The inner circle of the wheel connects colors of low chroma or dull intensity, such as gray-yellow and gray-green; the outer circle connects colors of full chroma or high intensity. One color used at full chroma combines harmoniously with its grayed equivalent at low chroma. For example, orange and gray-orange go well together.

Using Color

Any one or more of the above described relationships between colors can be exploited to advantage in a costume, depending on the effect desired.

While primary colors are quickly tiring to the eye and do not combine harmoniously, they are initially eye-catching in combination and can be effectively used to shock and even annoy the eye of the viewer. The most obvious kind of villain can be clad in primary red and black or black and yellow; the broadest kind of comic fool can wear red and green.

The cool colors generally give the effect of calm and rest, but they can also give a feeling of cold distance and may even be forbidding. Warm colors are exciting and loud, but they can lack subtlety. The warm colors advance, the cool colors recede. A costume which has a warm color predominating over a cool color is likely to be stronger than one which is made largely of a cool color.

Any two complementary colors provide both warmth and coolness in a harmonious, generally pleasing combination. The effect is even more pleasing if the complements are grayed, or if varying values are used. Also pleasing are three-color costumes using split complementary harmony. Equally harmonious are combinations of related values and intensities, as noted above.

If many bright colors are used in a costume, a large amount of black should be used also. Black unifies bright colors and tends to make them harmonious.

Finally, so-called Japanese color harmony makes colors seem unified and harmonious with a transparent or semi-transparent cloth over the whole costume. Or, in the same way, thin materials of various colors can be placed over a single, relatively strong color, thus relating all colors in a harmony keyed to the color showing through.

Harmony in a costume can also be achieved through line and pattern. A graceful silhouette fitted well to the body can give a pleasing effect. Luxurious, smoothly folding, or otherwise attractive fabrics arranged in a pleasing pattern can also add to the harmonious effect.

But harmony is not the sole objective of every costume. And not all costumes are designed to be seen alone.

Context

The first consideration in the designing of any costume must be the context or general situation within which it is to be worn. This will then determine, not only considerations of line, pattern and color, but such equally important matters as cost, durability, authenticity, and opportunity for abstraction and other imaginative experimentation.

Most costumes are worn in one of three different contexts: 1) as individual dress for Halloween or other holidays, or for masquerade balls or private costume affairs; 2) as costumes for performers in pageants or tableaux; 3) as dress for performers or actors on the stage.

Masquerades

There is usually no need for a masquerade or Halloween costume to harmonize with any other costume. Authenticity is not usually of vital concern, and there is often room for imaginative experimentation. Because such a costume is usually worn only once, materials need not be the most expensive, and work need not be the best. On the other hand, since the costume will be seen up close, detail and finish are fairly important. Comfort is a consideration if the costume is to be put to long or strenuous use. For children's Halloween costumes, safety is important. Materials should be non-flammable; weapons should be harmless; skirts and sashes should be designed so as not to cause the wearer to stumble; hats and masks should not dangerously obstruct visibility, because trick-or-treaters wander about in traffic, sometimes after sunset.

Pageants

Durability of fabric and sewing is not usually important in costuming a pageant, as it usually involves only a few performances. Detail and finish are usually not of vital concern for the same reason, and because the audience is usually at some distance. Authenticity can be important, since most pageants are historical in theme. Overall integration of design and color harmony are vitally important, since most pageants depend for their effect on large groups of people, seen as moving blocks of color. The appearance of the costumes under theatrical lighting can also be important, if the pageant is to be staged at night.

Stage

One of the most important considerations in designing a costume for the stage is the nature of the play or performance itself. An historical play obviously calls for more authentic costumes than a vaudeville revue. A revue generally calls for costumes of gayer and more colorful aspect, and often leaves room for more imaginative design. The nature of each character in a play dictates to some degree the nature of his costume. At the same time, the costumes must be integrated to fit the general theme and mood of the play. As certain characters will be weaker and others stronger, so certain costumes should emphasize in a positive or negative way, while others minimize and subordinate their wearers. Like the pageant, the play can be given an overall color scheme or tone. It is common, for instance, to key all the costumes in one scene to a given color harmonic, such as violet, with its complements, while reserving the reds and oranges for the leading character and associates—such as a king and his entourage. For the better plays, the scenery is designed to join the costuming in supporting the overall theme or quality of the intended performance.

Line, pattern, color, durability and authenticity can all be important in the stage costume. Keep in mind that the stage is an artificial situation. Costumes which look good enough close-up and under normal room lights or daylight can become formless and faded when seen under stage lights, from the audience.

Line is vitally important, as the silhouette of the costume is likely to make a deeper impression than pattern and even color. Pattern is important, however, and simplicity is the keynote; keep the units of the design as bold and clean-cut as possible. Texture of fabrics is not quite so important; detail can be kept to a minimum. From beginning to end, keep the context in mind. When buying fabrics, step back at least thirty feet to see if the texture and pattern "read" at a distance; that is, make the same effect at a distance as they do close-up. Try fabrics under stage lighting whenever possible. Try out the costumes periodically as you are working, placing your model against a strong light to test the effectiveness of the silhouette line. Check the overall pattern from a distance to see if excessively elaborate detail is confusing the general effect. In pattern as in line, simplicity is always best.

The same goes for color. Generally speaking, in all costumes, no more than two colors should be allowed to predominate, although other colors can be present. Choose color harmony or disharmony in accordance wtih considerations of individual character and the overall nature and intent of the play.

The importance of durability of fabric and work depends to a great degree on compromise between the number of performances anticipated and the amount of money available. The matter of the actor's comfort is also important; no actor can put in his best performance in too-tight breeches or with a safety pin pricking him every time he raises his arm. There can be no compromise when quick changes are demanded by the script; hooks and eyes should be strong and securely fastened; use zippers whenever possible, for security and speed.

The degree of authenticity required depends on the nature of the play, but should be consistent; if one costume has been carefully researched and meticulously patterned after its historical or ethnic counterpart, the same should be done with other costumes in the same play. It is a general rule that authenticity on the stage is less important than the overall effect of line, pattern and color; usually the purpose is less to educate the audience than to elicit an emotional reaction from them.

Basic Principles

The general rules of costume design can now be summarized:

The effectiveness of a costume depends on proper use of line, pattern, and color.

Restraint and simplicity are usually more effective than excess and complexity.

Each costume must meet both the requirements of the over-all performance, and those of the individual character or performer.

All costumes should be integrated with one another to meet the overall requirements of the presentation or play.

When a choice must be made between authenticity and emotional impact, the choice should be for emotional effectiveness.

Of course, these principles, along with others, are made to be broken, to a degree, and to a purpose.

Creative Design

The word "imaginative" means "to be full of images, fancies," and implies that those images are unusual, unique. To create new images you must try new and unusual approaches. Because primary colors do not readily harmonize does not mean that you cannot use them to create a kind of "clashing harmony" of reds for a devil's costume that will command the kind of agitated attention an arch demon deserves. Because the simplest design is usually the most effective does not mean you cannot create a "simple-complex" of bewildering patches for a comic hobo dancer.

The impression of authenticity does not always depend upon exact reproduction of a particular folk or historical costume. The body mask of a New Guinea war dancer need not be exactly faithful to the original straw version, but can be made of cellophane raffia to give an even more alien and exotic aspect. The silhouette or line of the medieval woman's dress, with long bliaut sleeves and pointed headdress, can be faithfully reproduced, but with an entirely original arrangement of color and pattern, to costume Snow White's stepmother.

Just because the costumes of the characters in *Alice in Won-*

derland are usually patterned after the original illustrations for that book does not mean that the March Hare, the Chesh-ire Cat, and the Queen of Hearts cannot be dressed in clothes that better fit your own fancy.

Learn the conventions, then break them in your mind. Re-

arrange the expected, changing commonly used line, pattern
and color. Try sketching your ideas out on paper. Imagine
them in use in the particular context you have in mind. Keep
an eye out for new materials, new fabrics such as vinyl and the
acetates, odds and ends of contemporary apparel, packaging

and hardware that might be put to effective use. Practice makes perfect. Read the play which follows this chapter, then devote some time to an exercise in creative thinking. Design and plan the costumes for Pyramus, Thisbe, Wall, Moonshine and Lion. And only then, when you have given your fancy a fling, turn the pages following the play and see how our designs compare with yours.

WALL, MOONSHINE AND LION

WALL, MOONSHINE
AND LION

A CLOWN INTERLUDE

adapted from A *Midsummer Night's Dream*
by William Shakespeare

Characters:

QUINCE . . . . speaker of the Prologue

PYRAMUS . . . . our hero

THISBY . . . . his lady love

WALL . . . . a wall

MOONSHINE . . . . the moon

LION . . . . a carnivore

Scene: A blank stage, empty as Quince declaims the Prologue. A box representing Old Ninny's grave can be put in place center stage for the final scene.

A NOTE ON THE PRODUCTION: *There is only one important prop: Thisby's mantle. It should be white, so that when Lion mauls it with his bloody teeth, the blood smears show bright red, convincing Pyramus that his love has met a grisly fate. A toy balloon full of red ink can be concealed in Lion's paw and popped under pressure to produce the bloody smears on the mantle. This is a clown play, one of Shakespeare's playful conceits, and it is meant to mean little if anything, as indicated in the Prologue. All characters are clowns and can wear clown make-up and clownish clothing. Pyramus is a comic version of the tragic hero, and his readiness to believe that his love has been eaten by a lion, followed by his headlong suicide, must be played as the absurdity it is, for fun, nonsense and laughter.*

Enter Quince

QUINCE: If we offend, it is with our good will.
    That you should think, we come not to offend,
But with good will. To show our simple skill,
    That is the true beginning of our end.
Consider, then, we come but in despite.
    We do not come, as minding to content you . . .
The actors are at hand; and, by their show,
You shall know all, that you are like to know.

Exit Quince. Enter Wall.

WALL: In this same interlude it doth befall
That I, one Snout by name, present a wall;
And such a wall, as I would have you think,
That had in it a crannied hole or chink,
Through which the lovers, Pyramus and Thisby,
Did whisper often very secretly.
This loam, this rough-cast, and this stone, doth show
That I am that same wall; the truth is so:
And this—(*holds up a hand with thumb and fore-
    finger circled to represent crack or hole*)—the
    cranny is, right and sinister,
Through which the fearful lovers are to whisper.

Enter Pyramus

PYRAMUS: O grim-look'd night! O night with use so black!
O night, which ever art when day is not!
O night, O night! alack, alack, alack,
I fear my Thisby's promise is forgot!
And thou, O wall, O sweet, O lovely wall,
That stand'st between her father's ground and mine!
Thou wall, O wall, O sweet and lovely wall!
Show me thy chink, to blink through with mine eyne.

Wall holds up his hand, the fingers circled to represent the chink.

PYRAMUS: Thanks, courteous wall: Jove shield thee well for this!
But what see I? No Thisby do I see.
O wicked wall, through whom I see no bliss!
Cursed be thy stones for thus deceiving me!

(*He petulantly whacks the wall, which winces.*)

Enter Thisbe from opposite side of stage.

THISBE: (*Caressing the wall from her side*)
O wall, full often hast thou heard my moans,
For parting my fair Pyramus and me!
My cherry lips have often kiss'd thy stones,
Thy stones with lime and hair knit up in thee.

PYRAMUS: (*Excited, peering through the chink from his side*)
I see a voice: now will I to the chink,
To spy an I can hear my Thisby's face.
Thisby!

THISBE: (*Peering through the chink from her side*)
My love! thou art my love, I think.

PYRAMUS: Think what thou wilt, I am thy lover's grace;
And, like Limander, am I trusty still.

THISBE: And I like Helen, till the Fates me kill.

PYRAMUS: O, kiss me through the hole of this vile wall!

THISBE: I kiss the wall's hole, not your lips at all.

As they try to kiss through the chink, Wall squirms, being ticklish.

PYRAMUS: (*desperately*) Wilt thou at Ninny's tomb meet me straightway?

THISBE: (*promising yes*) 'Tide life, 'tide death, I come without delay.

They exit in opposite directions, excitedly.

WALL: (*With evident relief*)
Thus have I, Wall, my part discharged so;
And, being done, thus Wall away doth go.

Exit Wall.

Lights briefly dim to indicate change of scene; box representing Ninny's tomb is placed center stage. Lights up.

Enter Lion and Moonshine.

LION: You, ladies, you, whose gentle hearts do fear
The smallest monstrous mouse that creeps on floor,
May now perchance both quake and tremble here,
When lion rough in wildest rage doth roar.

He roars, but ridiculously, choking at the end.

MOON: All that I have to say, is, to tell that the lantern is the moon; (*he turns on his lantern*) I, the man i' the moon; this thorn-bush, my thorn-bush; and this dog, my dog. (*He takes up a position off to the side*)

Enter Thisbe

THISBE: This is old Ninny's tomb. Where is my love?

LION: Oh well ... (*He lets out his most fearsome, most ridiculous roar.*)

Thisbe screams and runs off, leaving her mantle behind her. Lion continues to roar, carried away. He pounces on Thisbe's mantle, tearing at it, leaving it bloody. He then exits.

Enter Pyramus

PYRAMUS: Sweet Moon, I thank thee for thy sunny beams;
I thank thee, Moon, for shining now so bright;
For, by thy gracious, golden, glittering gleams
   I trust to take of truest Thisby sight.

(*He sees the bloody mantle, picks it up*)

   But stay, O spite!
   But mark, poor knight,
What dreadful dole is here!

(*He holds the mantle up*)

   Eyes, do you see?
   How can it be?
O dainty duck! O dear!
   Thy mantle good,
   What, stain'd with blood!
Approach, ye Furies fell!
   O Fates, come, come,
   Cut thread and thrum;
Quail, crush, conclude, and quell!

(*He staggers about, waving the bloody mantle,*

*playing it to the hilt, while Moonshine stands
blandly by, holding his lantern and looking bored)*

O wherefore, Nature, didst thou lions frame?
  Since lion vile hath here deflower'd my dear:
Which is—no, no, what *was* the fairest dame
    That lived, that loved, that liked, that look'd with
      cheer.

*(Weeping copiously, he draws his dagger and
poises it over his breast, still holding the mantle in
the other hand)*

    Come, tears, confound;
    Out, sword, and wound . . .
Thus die I, thus, thus, thus.

*(He stabs himself and falls, tangled in the bloody
mantle; but he is not quite dead yet.)*

    Now am I dead;
    Now am I fled;
My soul is in the sky *(he points upward)*
    Tongue, lose thy light;
    Moon, take thy flight:
Now die, die, die, die, die.

*He dies, as Moonshine looks on, bored, holding the
lantern. After a pause, Thisbe enters, approaches
the fallen Pyramus.*

THISBE: Asleep, my love?
    What, dead, my dove?
O Pyramus, arise!
    Speak, speak. Quite dumb?

*(She falls to her knees beside him, fully the ham
he was)*

Dead, dead? A tomb
Must cover thy sweet eyes.
  These lily lips,
  This cherry nose, (*She caresses his face*)
These yellow cowslip cheeks,
  Are gone, are gone:
  Lovers, make moan:
His eyes were green as leeks.

(*Ranting to her climax*)

  O Sisters Three,
  Come, come to me,
With hands as pale as milk;
  Lay them in gore,
  Since you have shore
With shears his thread of silk.

(*She puts a finger to her lips, draws her dagger*)

  Tongue, not a word:
  Come, trusty sword;
  Come, blade, my breast imbrue:

She stabs herself and falls across his body, address-
ing the audience.

  And farewell, friends;
  Thus Thisby ends:
Adieu, adieu, adieu.

She dies. After a long pause, Moonshine looks
around, as if to be sure there is no more to come,
then glances at the audience, shrugs, reaches up
and turns out his lantern.

Darkness as curtain.

Novelty
Costumes

As FURTHER encouragement to the costumer's imagination, here is a small collection of exotic and unusual costumes, some of them long popular, some long neglected, some entirely new. The costumer who has come this far is ready to exercise his own ingenuity and skills, and so in most cases complete instructions are not given.

88. CAT GIRL

This popular costume can be made from one-piece pajamas or tight coveralls of spotted, striped or solid-color material. For a more sultry effect, a black bathing suit or leotard can be worn with black tights, with the stuffed tail attached behind. The tail can be limp or made to hold a curled position by insertion of a wire core. The hood is like an aviator cap or hood (see No. 44) with a small cape or ruff at the bottom, to be tucked into the neck of the main garment. A few lines with an eyebrow pencil can simulate catlike eyes and whiskers. A Halloween mask can be purchased, or a half-mask made of papier-mâché, with pipe cleaner whiskers added. Ears are cut after the pattern shown, A, with a pleat cut into the lower edge to make

A

$3\frac{1}{2}''$

$4\frac{1}{2}''$

$3\frac{1}{2}''$

$8\frac{1}{2}''$

B

the ear concave. Rabbit ears are longer, B. Other animal costumes can be made along the same lines: squirrel, bear, fox.

89. CROCODILE

In the story of Peter Pan, the crocodile swallows the alarm clock, which alerts Captain Hook and the rest to his presence. The head can be made of construction board, finished with Claycrete. It is made in two pieces, top and bottom jaws. The body garment can be pajamas or coveralls, with a large tail attached, either stuffed with wadded up newspapers or shaped by hollow cardboard inserts. Hands and feet can be covered by taloned paws, made of matching material, with wooden or Claycrete claws. The whole costume can be given its rough texture by the application of sculpted squares of Claycrete. Or rolled tubes of crepe paper can be tied to the body garment at regular intervals, as illustrated. Using a similar two-unit principle, a head can be constructed of cardboard and papier-mâché for a large-billed bird, and a plumed body costume made to match.

90. MERMAID

From the waist up, she is a normal girl, but from the waist down she is something else again. The closed "skirt" is made in the shape of a fish's nether end, and of course limits her movement to a now and then fishy wriggle from her perch. She wears a swimsuit top with seashells (scallop shells are best) attached. The fishtail can be made from heavy buckram or canvas, sewed together and painted, or coated with green glitter or aluminum foil scales. Or it could be cast in latex, either over a canvas foundation or entirely of liquid rubber.

Casting Latex

Latex is an excellent material for casting flexible costume parts and accessories, such as hats and helmets, horns and antlers, "leather" parts, masks, and simulated armor. However, it is a difficult and expensive material to work with, and a full description of the process is unfortunately beyond the scope of this book. Complete instructions are available from the several manufacturers of latex. (Most large art supply stores carry latex materials. See also the author's *101 Masks*.)

91. DAISY

It is no great trick to become a pretty flower, but the elaboration of details can be fun and a real challenge. Here, a cloth hood is surrounded with petals cut from colored construction board or fairly stiff vinyl. Large leaves are also made of colored paper or vinyl and sewed or stapled to the flower "stalk"—the body of the wearer encased in tight-fitting green overalls or tights. All kinds of artificial leaves, flowers and vines can be purchased at display stores and even at the dime store.

92. TREE

You can become a whole tree by constructing a body mask of heavy canvas, twisted and painted to look like a gnarled trunk, with your arms inside canvas sleeves as the main branches. To finish, attach twigs, artificial foliage and a bird's nest.

93. QUARTER TO TWO

To become a clock, wear white tights and a white shirt with black sleeves. Construct a large clock dial out of heavy construction board and strap it to your back with shoulder straps. Now, by either manipulating two black

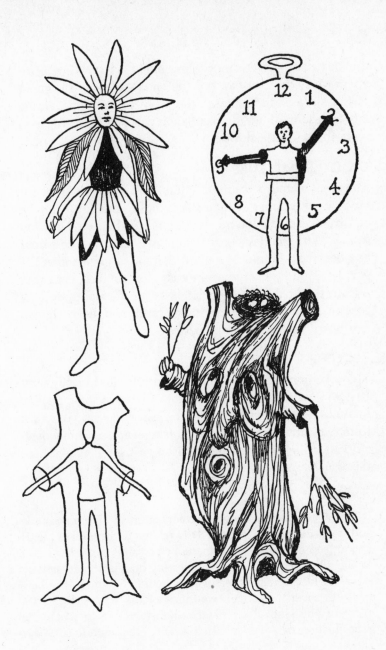

cardboard arrows, or simply stretching your arms out, sem-
aphore fashion, you can tell the time as you wish, going
fast or slow, as the fancy strikes you. If you happen to be
late for the masquerade party, you can point out that you
seem to be a little slow.

94. TOOTHPASTE TUBE

The constructed body mask offers endless possibilities for
novelty costuming. A man-sized toothpaste tube can be
constructed of cardboard with light wooden cross-bracing
inside. With similar construction methods, the costumer
can become a chimney, a giant domino, a giant index finger, etc. Holiday costumes are easy; for instance, construct
a giant, heart-shaped chocolate box for a Valentine's Day
costume. Or simply wear shorts and two heart-shaped
cardboard panels, front and back.

95. PSYCHEDELIC YOU

The variations are unlimited with pasties and body paint.
Paste-on costume accessories are available at some display
houses and costume shops, or you can make up your own
from bits of fluorescent paper, fringe and costume jewelry, attaching it to the body with spirit gum, available at
theatrical supply houses.

Body Paint

It is available in a range of colors from the large cosmetic
and theatrical supply houses. It is relatively expensive, but is
guaranteed non-toxic. Homemade body paints can be harmful
to the skin, and even the commercial brands should not be
worn for longer than three or four hours at a time. It is best
never to cover more than two-thirds of the skin surface with
paint of any kind. Body paint is indispensable for authentic
reproduction of American Indian and other aboriginal "war

paint." It is also necessary for simulating the decorative tattoo-ing worn by certain Japanese, New Zealand's Maori tribesmen, and the Marquesan islanders. When using body paint to recreate an elaborate design like that illustrated, it is best first to draw design outlines in black on the skin, then fill in the color. If body paint is not available, theatrical make-up colors can be used. They should, however, be thoroughly powdered; and even then, will tend to smear.

96. ELECTRIC LADY

Her elaborate gown is supported by a hoop skirt frame-work (see No. 64). Christmas tree lights can be attached, run off a hidden portable power pack, and caused to blink and wink alternately by use of a hidden hand switch or a solenoid. Special fluorescent fabrics can be used, and she can promenade or dance under black light, for a dazzling and eerie effect.

Black Light

The fluorescent paints, cloth and special lamps of theatrical black light are expensive, but can be very effective. A variety of costume materials are available at most theatrical supply houses, including sateens, gauzes and ready-made accessories, such as jewelry, feathers, hats. All glow with smoldering beauty under the special lights.

97. ROBOT

Here is another project for the accomplished amateur elec-trician. The body is made from a sturdy pasteboard box, reenforced, if necessary. Arms and legs can be sheathed in vinyl or canvas, wrapped with silver camera tape or sprayed with silver paint. Shoes can be silver-painted brogans on platform soles and heels. The head can be made from an inverted wastebasket or constructed with paste-

board. Hardware, electronic and otherwise, can then be
attached according to taste; and can even be made to oper-
ate, depending on the costumer's determination and skill.

98. HALF MAN—HALF WOMAN

Take two costumes, cut them down the middle, and combine the left half of one with the right half of the other.
(Or construct the hybrid from the ground up.) The costume can be featured as part of a backyard circus sideshow
or worn by a dancer appearing to dance with him (her?)
self. A variation would be a Doctor Jekyll and Mr. Hyde
costume, with one half representing the well-dressed and
ruthless Hyde, the other the frayed, kindly professor,
Jekyll.

Esoteric Costume Materials

A backyard circus sideshow might include such uncommon
costuming as the rough skin of the "alligator girl," which can
be reproduced by the use of collodion, also handy for making
fake scars, and is available at theatrical supply houses. Crepe
hair and spirit gum can be put to use to create a fearsome
wolfman or "wild man from Borneo," covered almost entirely
with hair. New and strange costume materials appear every
day, and can usually be found first at the larger theatrical
supply and window display houses.

99. INDIAN FAKIR

The snake actually dances and weaves to the piping of the
fakir's flute. He wears a version of Middle Eastern dress
described elsewhere (No. 81), but the trick is in the basket. It has a hole at the back, through which his left arm
passes, sheathed in the long cloth neck and papier-mâché
head of the snake puppet. The left arm of his jacket is
supported by an inner wire construction and stuffed with

cotton, with a false hand or stuffed glove at the end, appearing to hold the basket, which actually rests on the crooked inside of the elbow of the hidden arm. For security, the rear rim of the basket is sewed to the breast of the jacket. With his free right arm, the fakir plays the flute, while his left arm, inside the snake, sways and dances, hypnotized.

100. BREAKAWAY SUIT

This is an old vaudeville gag. It takes quite a bit of work to prepare for it, but it never fails to bring down the house. The objective is to reconstruct a suit of clothing so that it can be literally snatched off the performer's back. Choose an old suit or dress that fits the performer loosely, then take it apart. If it is a dress, undo the front seam or both side seams of the skirt, and the front seam or both side seams of the bodice. A high neck should be opened at the front. If the costume is a man's suit, the trousers should be opened up the inside seam of each leg and at the crotch, front and back. The coat should be opened down the seams of each arm. A dicky or false shirt front can be made of cardboard, or cut from the front of a dress shirt, with the tie added so that it looks normal, but is actually cut in two just under the collar. Once the parts of the costume are suitably separated, they should be sewed back as they were, but with long stitches of single thread. When the costume is assembled, stout nylon fishing line is attached to each major part from behind: a line each to right and left sleeves, one to the back of the jacket, one to the collar of the dicky, one each to the legs of the trousers, etc. All these nylon lines are then gathered into a bundle and held in the hand of someone back stage, preferably someone concealed behind a curtain directly behind the performer.

The front curtain can rise to reveal the performer, or the performer can walk out onto the stage, with the nylon lines trailing along the floor behind him. At an appropriate cue from the performer, perhaps his promise to give a friend the clothes off his back, the backstage operator gives a mighty heave on the bundle of lines and, if all goes well, causes the clothing to literally disappear from the performer's person, leaving him in the most basic costume of all: his birthday suit. Or, more properly, in some outlandish undergarment.

101. THE SWAMP

Here is the novelty costume to end all novelty costumes—
an appropriate end for this book. It is for use by not one,
but several costume party guests. It consists simply of an
old rug, preferably of dull, earthy color. It can be carried
rolled until needed. It is then unrolled and spread out on
the floor, whereupon the costumers all crawl underneath,
are quiet a moment, then begin to move their heads and
limbs fitfully, making the surface appear to be bubbling,
while at the same time giving out muffled sounds, as of a
swamp steaming and stewing in its own juice: blurb,
burble, blop, bloop.

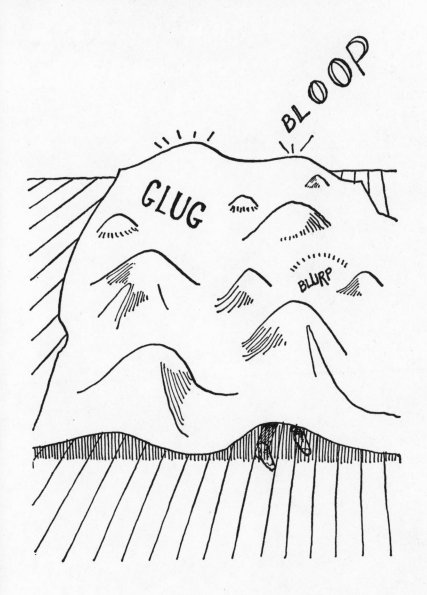

Index